The
Precious® Moments
Collector's Guide
to
COMPANY DOLLS

John & Malinda Bomm

COLLECTOR BOOKS
A Division of Schroeder Publishing Co., Inc.

Front cover:

Top row, left to right: #1228 Crystal, #1616 Bianca, #1074 Sarah, #1619 Keely, #1003 Missy.

Second row, left to right: #1378 Lollipop, #1145 Barbara Johnson, #1127 Charity, #1040 Chapel Fan Doll.

Bottom row, left to right: #1147 Jeremy, #2002 Carrie, #1510 Sulu, #1439 Angela, Timmy the Angel, #1214 Happy, #1441 Cindy.

Book design by Mary Ann Hudson

COLLECTOR BOOKS
P.O. Box 3009
Paducah, Kentucky 42002-3009

www.collectorbooks.com

Copyright © 2004 Precious Moments, Inc.
Licensee: Collector Books

The current values in this book should be used only as a guide. They are not intended to set prices, which vary from one section of the country to another. Auction prices as well as dealer prices vary greatly and are affected by condition as well as demand. Neither the authors nor the publisher assumes responsibility for any losses that might be incurred as a result of consulting this guide.

Searching For A Publisher?

We are always looking for people knowledgeable within their fields. If you feel that there is a real need for a book on your collectible subject and have a large comprehensive collection, contact Collector Books.

CONTENTS

ACKNOWLEDGMENTS

We would like to thank our mother for all the input, information collecting, and phone calling she had to do to make this book possible. She spent many, many hours of work helping put this book together.

An extra special thank you goes to Craig Schoehals, CEO of the Precious Moments Company and Ginnie Moore, also from the Precious Moments Company. Without their help this book would not have been completed. They have backed us up by sending us all the information they could find, beg, steal, or borrow from their vast library. We send a super thank you to both of them.

Thank you to Precious Moments collectors Marlene McKinnon, Tracey Waddell, and Brenda Miller for aiding us with pictures of dolls we could not find. With their help we have completed this book.

How To Use Your Precious Moments Price Guide

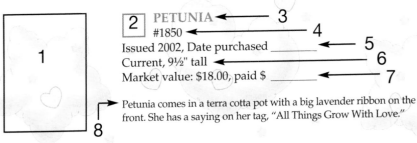

2 **PETUNIA** ← 3
#1850 ← 4
Issued 2002, Date purchased _____ ← 5
Current, 9½" tall ← 6
Market value: $18.00, paid $ _____ ← 7

Petunia comes in a terra cotta pot with a big lavender ribbon on the front. She has a saying on her tag, "All Things Grow With Love."

8

1. Photo – picture of the doll listed.

2. Checkbox for Inventory – box making it possible to keep track of personal collection.

3. Doll Name

4. Style Number – the quickest and most accurate means of identification for most of the dolls. The style number can be found on most of the dolls' tags.

5. Date of issue/ date purchased – lists the year the doll was manufactured and includes a blank in which the collector can write the date that the doll was bought.

6. Production status/ doll size – states whether the doll has been suspended or retired, was a limited edition, is closed, or is discontinued. This line also lists the size of the doll.

7. Market value/ purchase price – this line shows the cost of the item when found on the secondary market and includes a place for the collector to document the price that was paid for the doll.

8. Doll description – gives pertinent information about the doll.

ABOUT THE AUTHORS

John and Malinda Bomm are residents of Orlando, Florida. John was born in Amityville, New York in 1962. He, his younger brother, and parents stayed in New York until 1972 when his father was transferred to Pennsylvania. They lived in the beautiful Amish country area in Pennsylvania for three years until John's father was transferred again, this time to New Jersey. John completed his education in New Jersey and at the age of 16 started working for Pathmark Supermarkets as a cart boy and cashier. When John turned 18 he started building a race car, one of his passions through his growing years. Because of his race car building, John became top mechanic and worked with his parents in the service station they owned. John is now a warranty technician for one of the largest insurance companies in the country.

Malinda was born in 1962 on Naha Air Force Base in Okinawa, Japan. Her father was an Air Force Master Sergeant at the time. Her mother was a native of Okinawa. Malinda and her parents lived in Okinawa for nine years until they moved to Langley Air Force Base in Virginia. Malinda completed her education at Tabb High School in Virginia. Malinda moved to New Jersey in 1987 where she met future husband John. When John's parents moved to Florida, John and Malinda made the move with them. They were married on Valentine's Day, 1991. Malinda is now a health claims examiner for a large city agency.

Through Malinda, John developed a love of Precious Moments collectibles. Malinda and John's collection has expanded from five Precious Moments figurines to approximately 850 pieces, including bisque figurines, dolls, plates, water globes, and so much more. Several rooms in their house showcase their collection. This is their first Precious Moments book.

THE HISTORY OF SAM BUTCHER & PRECIOUS MOMENTS

Sam Butcher, creator of Precious Moments, has been able to help people all over the world. His figurines and their messages have touched the lives of countless individuals. Making their debut in 1978, Butcher's Precious Moments porcelain figurines fast became one of the top collectibles in the nation.

As a young child, Sam spent many an hour with his drawings. He had no desire to go out and play with his brothers and sister but his father insisted. His family was not wealthy but he was greatly blessed with a family full of love and Sam knows well that love is very important. Once a struggling evangelist, he moonlighted as a janitor to support his growing family. At a young age, he met Reverend Royal Blue, "who loves to tell the story." He was a great influence in Sam's life. Because of him Sam has had a heart full of love and joy. God has remained with him all his life.

Though he is one of America's most beloved artists, Sam has never forgotten his humble beginnings as a "Chalk Talks" minister, when he used illustrations to teach young children about God. With a strong spiritual commitment, he accepted a job as an artist at the International Child Evangelism Fellowship in Grand Rapids, Michigan. For 10 years, his work was seen by millions of viewers on the program "Tree Top House." During this time he also was the illustrator for Christian album covers and books.

Butcher, who now lives in the Philippine Islands, created the drawings of the teardrop-eyed children that inspired Precious Moments figurines when he and his partner at the time, Bill Biel, worked for the company Jonathan & David. Biel owned the company and both he and Butcher worked as commercial artists. Butcher states that they started by producing greeting cards. Eugene Freedman of the Enesco Corporation (makers of Precious Moments figurines) saw the artwork and asked the artists to have them produced in porcelain. As time went on, Biel's interest leaned toward administration while Butcher began designing for Precious Moments.

Sam's and Bill's success with the Enesco line has given them freedom to open their hearts to their Christian ministry. In 1985, they traveled to the Philippines and discovered a group of Bible school students in financial trouble. It was because of them that a line of Precious Moments dolls were produced. The first two dolls, Jesus Loves Me Boy and Girl, were manufactured. Their tags explain the reason for the company's purpose. It states:

"Deep in the heart of the Philippines, young Bible School students spend part of their day producing these "Jesus Loves Me" dolls. Without this financial assistance they would not be able to complete their education and go into their desired ministries. The Jonathan & David Company of the Philippines began in 1987 when Bill Biel and Sam Butcher became acquainted with a small Bible college in the city of Iloilo, located on the Panay Island. They discovered 33 students were dropping out of school due to the lack of sufficient funds. It was then that these two men decided to start a company for the sole purpose of supporting these students. These warm and beautiful dolls are the fruit of their labor. Carefully designed and produced with so much love, they are sure to win their way into the hearts of children everywhere."

The Jonathan & David Company produced nine Precious Moments dolls over a span of three years. They closed their doors in 1988.

Butcher says he came up with the characters as a type of ministry. "I really wanted to share the word of God in a very positive way with people. And, of course, we did that by the greeting cards and then the Precious Moments figurines, and now I've built a chapel in Missouri that's become a major tourist attraction." Many of his ideas are inspired by Bible verses, others by thought, and others by people.

In 1986, 5" dolls were made exclusively for the Samuel J. Butcher Company. These dolls were distributed in the United States by the Samson Company (Sam's two sons, Jon and Phillip). Because of Sam's semi-retirement, Jon devoted himself towards being spokesman for the Samuel J. Butcher Company while Sam spent his time walking and talking with the Lord. It was during this time that Sam turned his dreams into reality.

Precious Moments Country Incorporated, of Carthage, Missouri, a company owned by a member of the family, continued the vinyl doll line. This company eventually changed its name to Precious Moments Company. It continues to operate its telemarketing business and warehousing operations from Carthage. The company has recently streamlined its operation to concentrate on their ever-growing, increasingly popular line of collectible vinyl dolls.

When Precious Moments Company went online, Debbie, Sam Butcher's daughter, started working for the company designing dolls. "Children of the World," her first set of dolls, featured dolls from several nations. Another group called "Preferred Doll Retailers" was a special line of limited dolls only available to a certain group of retailers.

The "Classics" collection portrays beautifully crafted clothing made of lovely fabrics, lace, and ribbons. They were limited in production numbers and sold well to both retailers and collectors. They are fun dolls that capture the hearts of doll collectors as well as porcelain collectors. Both seem to enjoy their cute messages.

Precious Moments Company continues to manufacture beautiful limited edition dolls such as "Marcy," the Amway dolls, and the "Shonnie" Indian doll, which are a few of the must sought after dolls today. Many of the dolls are named after a particular person. The staff also comes up with names that are in keeping with the doll's theme or series, such as the Garden Friends or the Jewel dolls.

The entire process of producing a doll can take anywhere from three weeks to three months, depending on the difficulty of costumes and theme. This is the normal process for making a doll:

- The doll idea and name are agreed upon.
- The idea is transformed into artwork and given to the factory.
- The factory produces a prototype of the doll and returns it for approval.
- The prototype is reviewed for quality, accuracy, and detail. If necessary, changes are requested and a revised prototype is produced. The prototype is approved for production.

Many changes have occurred over the past ten years. PMC started with only 16" dolls. "Children of the World" dolls in 9" size were introduced in 1989. Now there are 4" and 7" dolls on the market.

Sam Butcher's Chapel opened its doors in 1987 and allows the tourist and collector to view Precious Moments characters on stained glass, bronze plates, woodcarvings, and other forms. Building his Chapel in 1989 was, as he states, "an inspiration from the Lord." It is located on hundreds of acres of rolling hills and farmland in Carthage, Missouri.

The Chapel, featuring a Precious Moments version of Michelangelo's "Creation," draws nearly one million visitors annually. It contains more than 50 Precious Moments Renaissance colored murals, 30 stained glass windows, two nine-foot bronze sculptures, 350-pound, hand-carved wooden doors, galleries with personal tributes and a gift shop. The 25th anniversary celebration for the collection is being planned for 2003. Sam Butcher continues to create improvements to the art collections of the Precious Moments Chapel.

Sam has received many accolades for his artistic achievements. In 1988, he received a Special Recognition Award from the National Association of Limited Edition Dealers (NALED) and in 1992 and 1996 he was named "Artist of the Year" by NALED.

Precious Moments Country, Inc. was changed over to Precious Moments Company, Inc., in 1992. The doors of this company remain open today and continue to expand the doll industry.

Today the Butcher family takes an active roll in the company. One of Sam's sons is the manager of the company, one daughter is a writer, and the other son is an artist. When Sam is not traveling in this country, he can be found in the Philippines working in his studio or performing his ministry where he supports Bible school students and helps get children off the streets and into homes. He plans someday to write about his life and travel experiences, a book that he will author himself.

DOLL TAGS

Jonathan & David, Inc. produced only nine 16" dolls. The front of the 1¾" x 3¼" white tag depicts two angels on a cloud, "But Love Goes On Forever." Inside the tag, you will find the doll's name with a special message to the collector: *"Deep in the heart of the Philippines, young Bible school students spend a part of their day producing these 'Happiness in the Lord' dolls. Without this financial assistance they would not be able to complete their education and go into their desired ministries. The Jonathan & David Company of the Philippines began in 1987 when Bill Biel and Sam Butcher became acquainted with a small Bible college in the city of Iloilo, located on the Panay Island. They discovered 33 students who were dropping out of school due to the lack of sufficient funds. It was then that these two men decided to start a company for the sole purpose of supporting these students. These warm and beautiful dolls are the fruit of their labor. Carefully designed and produced with so much love, they are sure to win their way into the hearts of children everywhere."*

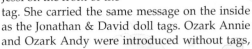

In 1989, Precious Moments Country, Inc., changed all the white tags to measure 2⅝" x 3¼". The Blue Missy and Pink Missy had a picture of a Precious Moments girl holding a bouquet of flowers with "Missy" on the front of it. She carried the same message on the inside as the Jonathan & David doll tags.

The bride doll Jessi, which was introduced in 1989, had a picture of a bride and Jessi on the front of the tag. She carried the same message on the inside as the Jonathan & David doll tags. Ozark Annie and Ozark Andy were introduced without tags, but shortly thereafter they were given miniature doll catalog tags.

The 2⅛" x 2¾" white tag had the girl with a goose on the front of it but no name. The message inside of the tag is *"It is without question that Asia's finest sewers are found in the Philippine Islands."*

"When Mr. Samuel Butcher visited the Philippines for the first time, he was greatly impressed by the skill of Hongos in the region of Panay. As a result, he established a factory that offered work for needy students and provided Precious Moments dolls for the states. However, because of a growing demand for the dolls, he later transferred to Manila to better accommodate the orders. Now to continue with his desire to provide education to the needy, much of the Precious Moments Dolls' revenue is used to provide scholarships and vocational opportunities for students throughout the country."

In 1989, Precious Moments Country, Inc., introduced the 9" dolls for the ongoing series, Children of the World. They were first introduced without tags, but in 1991 they were given miniature catalog Children of the World tags. In 1993, they were given individual satchel tags with their own names on them.

In 1992, the dolls began to carry the year they were produced. This helps identify Children of the World dolls that have been in production over the past five years. The date is imprinted on the doll's back, neck, or hairline. Prior to this time, it read, *"Made in the Philippines, Precious Moments, Samuel Butcher Co. USA."*

All dolls began to have their own individual tags in 1993. Many times the doll tag will give you additional information concerning the doll. For example, Casey, the Precious Moments baseball player, is not dressed in the usual burgundy and white Precious Moments Chapel colors. Casey was born on July 4, and he is wearing the appropriate colors for that day. The Jessi and Baby Lisa tag is unique as it carries Baby Lisa's birth certificate on the inside. Phillip has a certificate that can be framed for display.

The Native American doll collection tag is also a certificate that is found on the inside of the tag. At the bottom of this certificate the doll's number in the line of production is given.

The Lindsay and Dustin doll tags have the pictures of the real children on them. These dolls were available only at the Chapel, and were made for the 1995 Christmas Collector's Weekend.

The Garden of Friends series has a "watering can" tag, stating 1st, 2nd, or 3rd edition. The tag gives the month, doll's name, and the saying, "Where friendship blooms forever."

The Precious Jewels collection tag features a foil stamp to match the color of the jewel. Sam's biblical interpretation of the gem is on the inside of the tag.

The following animals wear a white oval plastic tag embossed in gold (15" and 21"): Charlie Bear, Letty Bear, Landon Bear, Edmond Bear, Eyvette Bear, Grant Bear In Stocking, and Bailey Bunny. There are seven animals in current production that wear white oval paper tags (48"): Charlie, Bride Bear, Groom Bear, Snowball Bear With Vest, Parker Plaid Bear, Dillon Denim Bear, and Colton Corduroy Bear.

The Precious Pals debuted in September 1997. Six animals were chosen from the Precious Moments videos to begin the series. They have a 1" x 1" blue and white tag. Inside the tag is a poem for each animal and tells what video the animal represents. The back of the tag states the name and item number.

Gil The Fish is a special Precious Pal given to collectors who registered for the 1997 Licensee Event in July-August 1997. He was limited to 1,750 pieces and was completely distributed. Gil has a 1" x 2" white and blue tag with Gil's poem on the back.

CLEANING TIPS

Remember that these beautiful dolls were made to be toys for children. They are certainly durable enough to be put on display. Take them out of their boxes and bags and show them off!

Vinyl doll body parts get dirty just from handling. Try cleaning the spots with mild soap and water. Pen marks or permanent ink can possibly be removed by using a pencil's eraser. If that doesn't work, put a dab of polish remover on a cotton swab or a Q-tip. Be extremely careful around the eyes of the doll.

Doll clothing can be hand washed if needed. Delicate material can be spot washed with a good spot remover. The new dry cleaning products can also be used to remove dust and lint. Periodically use your hair blower to remove the light dust. Use the dryer on air only.

Most of the dolls were produced to be played with; therefore, they have rooted hair. Gently brush or comb the hair with a vented brush or comb or use a pick. You may wash it in a mild shampoo and style it with pin curls. Using a pick will increase the height and restore the curls.

Display your dolls in a cabinet, under glass or in plastic domes on doll stands. Keep them away from strong sunlight and really bright lights. Don't use strong lights in curio cabinets. These strong lights can fade clothing and hair and possibly burn holes in your dolls and their clothing if they are too close to the hot lights. Keep them away from your kitchen or cooking area where there is grease, which is very hard on the dolls and their hair.

If purchasing a doll from the secondary market, make sure to check for faded hair and clothing. Check the fabric under the arms and front from the back to make sure they are the same color. Check the hair under a hat and see if both are the same coloring. Turn the doll upside down and check to see if the bottom hair is the same color as the top. Make sure it has a Certificate of Authenticity if it came with one.

Bring your special doll home, display, and enjoy it!

ALL THINGS GROW WITH LOVE

☐ **PETUNIA**
#1850
Issued 2002, Date purchased _____
Current, 9½" tall
Market value: $18.00, paid $_____

Petunia comes in a terra cotta pot with a big lavender ribbon on the front. She has a saying on her tag, "All Things Grow With Love."

☐ **PETALS**
#1851
Issued 2002, Date purchased _____
Current, 9½" tall
Market value: $18.00, paid $_____

Petals comes in a terra cotta pot with a big pink ribbon on the front. She has a saying on her tag, "Love Is In Bloom."

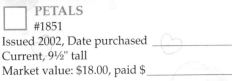

☐ **SUNNY**
#1852
Issued 2002, Date purchased _____
Current, 9½" tall
Market value: $18.00, paid $_____

Sunny comes in a terra cotta pot with a big yellow ribbon on the front. She has a saying on her tag, "Stop & Smell the Flowers."

☐ **DAISY**
#1853
Issued 2002, Date purchased _____
Current, 9½" tall
Market value: $18.00, paid $_____

Daisy comes in a terra cotta pot with a big yellow ribbon on the front. She has a saying on her tag, "Seeds Of Love."

ALWAYS IN MY HEART

☐ **JULIANNE**
#1329
Issued 1999, Date purchased _____
Current, 12" tall
Market value: $29.50, paid $_____

Julianne is dressed in a pretty white and red dress with
pearls and tiny white rosettes. She is carrying a lace purse
and wearing white lace pantyhose and white shoes.

☐ **MAKAYLA**
#1350
Issued 2000, Date purchased _____
Current, 12" tall
Market value: $29.50, paid $_____

Makayla wears a black, white, and red outfit accented
with red hearts. She has brunette hair pulled into
ponytails.

☐ **PAYTON**
#1369
Issued 2001, Date purchased _____
Current, 12" tall
Market value: $29.50, paid $_____

Payton is dressed in a nice pink and white satin dress and has
a pink ribbon in her hair. Payton is third in the series.

ALWAYS MY LITTLE GIRL

Each doll features a golden heart-shaped pendant.

BABY IN BASSINET
#1637
Issued 1998, Date purchased _____
Current, 4" tall
Market value: $11.95, paid $ _____

This cute tiny doll is the first edition in the "Always My Little Girl" Series.

TODDLER
#1638
Issued 1998, Date purchased _____
Current, 7" tall
Market value: $12.95, paid $ _____

This cute 7" doll is the second edition in the "Always My Little Girl" Series.

FIRST DAY OF SCHOOL
#1566
Issued 1999, Date purchased _____
Current, 9" tall
Market value: $21.00, paid $ _____

This cute 9" doll is the third edition in the "Always My Little Girl" Series.

SUNDAY BEST
#1469
Issued 1999, Date purchased _____
Current, 12" tall
Market value: $30.00, paid $ _____

This pretty 12" doll is the fourth edition in the "Always My Little Girl" Series.

SLUMBER PARTY
#1495
Issued 1999, Date purchased _____
Suspended 2001, 12" tall
Market value: $30.00, paid $ _____

This fifth edition in the "Always My Little Girl" Series represents the days of youth and fun slumber parties.

SWEET 16
#1136
Issued 1999, Date purchased _____
Suspended 2001, 12" tall
Market value $45.00, paid $ _____

This 16" doll is the sixth and final edition in the "Always My Little Girl" Series.

AMWAY SERIES

☐ **JESSICA**
#1028
Issued 1991, Date purchased _____
Limited 3,000, 16" tall
Market value: $575.00 – 625.00, paid $ _____

Jessica is the first edition in the Amway series. She wears a pink and tan flowered print old-fashioned dress, which is trimmed in pink ribbons and white lace. In her hair are matching pink satin ribbons.

☐ **MELISSA**
#1033
Issued 1992, Date purchased _____
Limited 4,000, 16" tall
Market value: $250.00 – 275.00, paid $ _____

Melissa is the second edition in the Amway series. She is dressed in a red, green, and white Christmas dress with white lace on the bottom. She has green ribbons in her hair making pigtails.

☐ **MADDY**
#1041
Issued 1994, Date purchased _____
Limited 6,000, 16" tall
Market value: $175.00 – 200.00, paid $ _____

Maddy is the fourth edition in the Amway Series. She is dressed in a light blue top and blue print skirt with a pink bow around her waistline. She is wearing a pink bow with blue and pink flowers in her hair.

☐ **REBECCA**
#1052
Issued 1993, Date purchased _____
Limited 5,000, 16" tall
Market value: $200.00 – 225.00, paid $ _____

Rebecca is the third edition in the Amway Series. She is dressed in a beautiful white gown, accented with pink trim around the sleeves, waistline, and neckline.

BRIANNA
#1059
Issued 1996, Date purchased _____
Limited 5,000, 16" tall
Market value: $125.00 – 150.00, paid $ _____

Brianna is the sixth edition in the Amway Series. She is dressed in white satin and bows. The neckline and skirt of the dress contain a rainbow of colors.

MARISSA
#1096
Issued 1995, Date purchased _____
Limited 4,500, 16" tall
Market value: $180.00 – 200.00, paid $ _____

Marissa is the fifth edition in the Amway Series. She is dressed in a pink satin bodice, with a pink and white floral skirt trimmed with lace. She has pink ribbons in her hair, around her neckline, and around her waist.

KATHERINE
#1111
Issued 1997, Date purchased _____
Limited 5,000, 16" tall
Market value: $75.00 – 100.00, paid $ _____

Katherine is the seventh doll in the Amway Series. She is dressed in a long green corduroy skirt with an ivory silk blouse. She has an ivory ribbon in her hair and is carrying a purse to match the skirt.

KIESHA
#1112
Issued 1997, Date purchased _____
Limited 2,500, 16" tall
Market value: $75.00 – 100.00, paid $ _____

Kiesha is the eighth doll in the Amway Series. She is dressed in a long green corduroy skirt with an ivory silk blouse. She has an ivory ribbon in her hair and is carrying a purse to match the skirt.

MERRY

Issued 1998, Date purchased _____
Limited 2,500, 16" tall
Market value: $50.00 – 75.00, paid $ _____

Merry is dressed in a cream blouse and plaid skirt. She has long curly brown hair with a ribbon in it.

BRANDI

Issued 1998, Date purchased _____
Limited 2,500, 16" tall
Market value: $50.00 – 75.00, paid $ _____

Brandi has long black hair with a ribbon in it. She is dressed in a beautiful red and white dress.

ANGELS OF THE MONTH

JANUARY
#4117
Issued October 2002, Date purchased _____
Current, 9" tall
Market value: $29.50, paid $_____

January has long curly blond hair. She is wearing a long blue gown accented with flowers. She has white feathered wings on her back.

FEBRUARY
#4118
Issued October 2002, Date purchased _____
Current, 9" tall
Market value: $29.50, paid $_____

February has long black hair with a pink ribon. She is wearing a long pink gown accented with flowers. She has white feathered wings on her back.

MARCH
#4119
Issued October 2002, Date purchased _____
Current, 9" tall
Market value: $29.50, paid $_____

March has long brown curly hair with a white halo. She is wearing a mint green gown with flower accents. She has white feathered wings on her back.

APRIL
#4120
Issued October 2002, Date purchased _____
Current, 9" tall
Market value: $29.50, paid $_____

April has long straight blond hair with a halo in it. She is dressed in a long pink gown accented with flowers. She has white feathered wings on her back.

MAY
#4121

Issued October 2002, Date purchased _____
Current, 9" tall
Market value: $29.50, paid $_____

May has long brown curly hair with a halo of flowers in it. She is dressed in a long lavender gown accented with flowers. She has white feathered wings on her back.

JUNE
#4122

Issued October 2002, Date purchased _____
Current, 9" tall
Market value: $29.50, paid $_____

June has long straight black hair with a white halo. She is dressed in a long white gown accented with flowers. She has white feathered wings on her back.

JULY
#4123

Issued Ocober 2002, Date purchased _____
Current, 9" tall
Market value: $29.50, paid $_____

July has long curly blond hair with a large teal ribbon in it. She is dressed in a long teal gown with flower accents. She has white feathered wings on her back.

AUGUST
#4124

Issued October 2002, Date purchased _____
Current, 9" tall
Market value: $29.50, paid $_____

August has long curly brown hair with a peach ribbon around her head. She is dressed in a long peach gown accented with flowers. She has white feathered wings on her back.

SEPTEMBER
#4125
Issued October 2002, Date purchased _____
Current, 9" tall
Market value: $29.50, paid $_____

September has long straight blond hair with a feathered halo on her head. She is dressed in a long cream gown accented with green flowers. She has white feathered wings on her back.

OCTOBER
#4126
Issued October 2002, Date purchased _____
Current, 9" tall
Market value: $29.50, paid $_____

October has long curly brown hair with a large tan bow halo. She is dressed in a long tan gown accented with flowers. She has white feathered wings on her back.

NOVEMBER
#4127
Issued October 2002, Date purchased _____
Current, 9" tall
Market value: $29.50, paid $_____

November has long curly blond hair with a white feathered halo with flower accents. She is dressed in a beautiful dark green gown accented with flowers. She has white feathered wings on her back.

DECEMBER
#4128
Issued October 2002, Date purchased _____
Current, 9" tall
Market value: $29.50, paid $_____

December has long curly black hair with a white halo with red bow. She is dressed in a long red gown accented with red flowers. She has white feathered wings on her back.

ANGELS OF VIRTUE

☐ **FAITH**
   #4236
Issued October 2002, Date purchased _____
Current, 12" tall
Market value: $42.00, paid $_____

Faith has long curly black hair accented with pink flowers.
She is wearing a long pink gown with ribbon and flower
accents. She has pink and white feathered wings on her back.

☐ **PATIENCE**
   #4237
Issued October 2002, Date purchased _____
Current, 12" tall
Market value: $42.00, paid $_____

Patience has long curly brown hair accented with white flowers.
She is wearing a long white gown accented with white ribbons
and flowers. She has white feathered wings on her back.

☐ **CHARITY**
   #4238
Issued October 2002, Date purchased _____
Current, 12" tall
Market value: $42.00, paid $_____

Charity has beautiful blond curly hair with pink flower
accents. She is wearing a long pink gown with pink ribbon
accents. She has pink wings on her back.

GARNET – JANUARY
#4201
Issued 2001, Date purchased _____
Current, 12" tall
Market value: $29.95, paid $_____

Garnet is dressed in a long blue gown trimmed in a gold tone. She is also wearing a matching cape. Her hair is styled in pigtails with blue ribbons.

AMETHYST – FEBRUARY
#4202
Issued 2001, Date purchased _____
Current, 12" tall
Market value: $29.95, paid $_____

Amethyst is dressed in a lavender and light blue dress, trimmed in satin lavender ribbons. She has her hair up in pigtails.

AQUAMARINE – MARCH
#4203
Issued 2001, Date purchased _____
Current, 12" tall
Market value: $29.95, paid $_____

Aquamarine has pretty curly blond hair with a blue ribbon. She wears an aquamarine and white sleeved dress with white lace on the bottom.

DIAMOND – APRIL
#4204
Issued 2001, Date purchased _____
Current, 12" tall
Market value: $29.95, paid $_____

Diamond has a red head of hair in pigtails. She models a white and pink print satin dress with pink trim.

EMERALD – MAY
#4205
Issued 2001, Date purchased _____
Current, 12" tall
Market value: $29.95, paid $_____

Emerald is clad in an emerald green dress with a printed top.
She has brunette hair that is tied up with a green ribbon. She is
wearing green shoes that match the dress.

PEARL – JUNE
#4206
Issued 2001, Date purchased _____
Current, 12" tall
Market value: $29.95, paid $_____

Pearl wears a yellow dress with pink trim and white laced bottoms.
She has in her red hair a yellow ribbon. She has a heart-shaped
charm around her neck.

RUBY – JULY
#4207
Issued 2001, Date purchased _____
Current, 12" tall
Market value: $29.95, paid $_____

Ruby is wearing a beautiful rose and white satin dress. She has
red hair tied up into pigtails with rose flowered ribbons.

PERIDOT – AUGUST
#4208
Issued 2001, Date purchased _____
Current, 12" tall
Market value: $29.95, paid $_____

Peridot has red hair pulled up into a bun with a white ribbon.
She is dressed in a white and light green satin dress, accented
with little roses.

SAPPHIRE – SEPTEMBER
#4209
Issued 2001, Date purchased _____
Current, 12" tall
Market value: $29.95, paid $_____

Sapphire wears a white, blue, and pink dress with a blue bow at the waistline. She has a blue ribbon in her brunette hair.

OPAL – OCTOBER
#4210
Issued 2001, Date purchased _____
Current, 12" tall
Market value: $29.95, paid $_____

Opal has pretty curly blond hair. She is dressed in a cream-colored top and multicolored bottom satin dress.

TOPAZ – NOVEMBER
#4211
Issued 2001, Date purchased _____
Current, 12" tall
Market value: $29.95, paid $_____

Topaz is a beautiful red-headed girl wearing a white and tan satin dress with big cuffs.

BLUE TOPAZ – DECEMBER
#4212
Issued 2001, Date purchased _____
Current, 12" tall
Market value: $29.95, paid $_____

This doll is dressed for Christmas in a green and multi colored dress. She is carrying a white muff.

AT THE RECITAL

☐ **TWINKLE**
  #4103
Issued August 2002, Date purchased _____
Current, 9" tall
Market value: $24.00, paid $_____

Twinkle has beautiful brown hair pulled up with white ribbons. She is dressed in a white ballerina tutu and purple dancing slippers.

☐ **TINKER**
  #4104
Issued August 2002, Date purchased _____
Current, 9" tall
Market value: $24.00, paid $_____

Tinker has beautiful blond hair pulled up with white ribbons. She is dressed in a pink ballerina tutu and pink dancing slippers.

☐ **TOOTSIE**
  #4105
Issued August 2002, Date purchased _____
Current, 9" tall
Market value: $24.00, paid $_____

Tootsie has black hair and white hair ribbons. She is dressed in a lavender tutu and matching dancing slippers.

AVON – SPECIAL EDITION

☐ **TIMMY THE ANGEL MUSICAL DOLL**

Issued 1999, Date purchased _____
Current, 16" tall
Market value: $50.00 – 75.00, paid $_____

Timmy is dressed in a blue angelic gown carrying a purple colored blanket. He has a golden halo on his head. On his back are his golden angel wings. He is a musical doll.

BERRY BEST FRIENDS COLLECTION

These little dolls are all soft cloth dolls as opposed to vinyl. They are wearing dresses with appliqué fruits on the fronts to coincide with their names. Strawberry's hair is up in ponytails. Boysenberry's hair has a lavender ribbon around it. Raspberry's hair has pink bows on the sides. Blueberry's hair is down.

STRAWBERRY
#1625
Issued 1996, Date purchased _____
Current, 14" tall
Market value: $29.95, paid $_____

BOYSENBERRY
#1628
Issued 1996, Date purchased _____
Current, 14" tall
Market value: $29.95, paid $_____

RASPBERRY
#1626
Issued 1996, Date purchased _____
Current, 14" tall
Market value: $29.95, paid $_____

BLUEBERRY
#1627
Issued 1996, Date purchased _____
Current, 14" tall
Market value: $29.95, paid $_____

BIRTHDAY BLESSINGS

☐ **JANUARY**
   #1351
Issued 2001, Date purchased _____
Current, 12" tall
Market value: $29.95, paid $ _____

January is dressed in a pretty red and black dress with lace around the neckline. She is carrying a little Precious Moments doll. She has red bows in her hair.

☐ **FEBRUARY**
   #1352
Issued 2001, Date purchased _____
Current, 12" tall
Market value: $29.95, paid $ _____

February is dressed in slacks and a printed blouse with lavender ribbons in her hair. She is carrying her favorite Precious Moments rag doll.

☐ **MARCH**
   #1353
Issued 2001, Date purchased _____
Current, 12" tall
Market value: $29.95, paid $ _____

March is wearing a light blue and flowered print dress and a pair of eyeglasses. On the top of each of her shoes is a yellow flower. She is carrying a little Precious Moments doll.

☐ **APRIL**
   #1354
Issued 2001, Date purchased _____
Current, 12" tall
Market value: $29.95, paid $ _____

April is dressed in a white sleeved and multicolored dress. She is carrying her favorite Precious Moments doll dressed to match her.

MAY
☐ #1355
Issued 2001, Date purchased _____
Current, 12" tall
Market value: $29.95, paid $_____

May is clad in a pretty tan and green printed dress with green shoes. On her head is a matching hat with a green bow on it. She is carrying her own Precious Moments doll.

JUNE
☐ #1356
Issued 2001, Date purchased _____
Current, 12" tall
Market value: $29.95, paid $_____

June is dressed in a pink, cream and flowered jumpsuit with a matching summer bonnet on her head. She is carrying her own Precious Moments rag doll.

JULY
☐ #1357
Issued 2001, Date purchased _____
Current, 12" tall
Market value: $29.95, paid $_____

This pretty little pigtailed blonde is ready for summer. She is wearing white-sleeved, red and white plaid, and flowered dress with little red shoes. She is carrying a Precious Moments doll dressed like her.

AUGUST
☐ #1358
Issued 2001, Date purchased _____
Current, 12" tall
Market value: $29.95, paid $_____

August is dressed in a green and flowered dress with matching flowered shoes. She is carrying a matching Precious Moments doll.

SEPTEMBER
#1359
Issued 2001, Date purchased _____
Current, 12" tall
Market value: $29.95, paid $_____

September is ready for the first day of school with her plaid skirt, white blouse, and red vest. She wears a pair of eyeglasses and a red ribbon in her hair. She is carrying a Precious Moments doll.

OCTOBER
#1360
Issued 2001, Date purchased _____
Current, 12" tall
Market value: $29.95, paid $_____

October is ready for the fall festival. She is dressed in a black jumper with a print blouse. In her hair is a pink ribbon. She is also carrying a Precious Moments doll.

NOVEMBER
#1361
Issued 2001, Date purchased _____
Current, 12" tall
Market value: $29.95, paid $_____

November wears a golden print and black jumpsuit with two big buttons on it. She has pretty red hair put up on the side of her head and is carrying her favorite Precious Moments doll.

DECEMBER
#1362
Issued 2001, Date purchased _____
Current, 12" tall
Market value: $29.95, paid $_____

December is prepared for winter in a heavy green and holly print dress with white fur accenting the sleeves and bottom of the dress. She is carrying a Precious Moments doll.

BIRTHDAY WISHES COLLECTION

These dolls are not made of vinyl, but soft cloth material instead. Each one's attire features colors often seen in their corresponding months.

JANUARY
#1951
Issued 1996, Date purchased _____
Discontinued 1998, 11" tall
Market value: $19.95, paid $_____

FEBRUARY
#1952
Issued 1996, Date purchased _____
Discontinued 1998, 11" tall
Market value: $19.95, paid $_____

MARCH
#1953
Issued 1996, Date purchased _____
Discontinued 1998, 11" tall
Market value: $19.95, paid $_____

APRIL
#1954
Issued 1996, Date purchased _____
Discontinued 1998, 11" tall
Market value: $19.95, paid $_____

☐ **MAY**
#1955
Issued 1996, Date purchased _____
Discontinued 1998, 11" tall
Market value: $19.95, paid $_____

☐ **JUNE**
#1956
Issued 1996, Date purchased _____
Discontinued 1998, 11" tall
Market value: $19.95, paid $_____

☐ **JULY**
#1957
Issued 1996, Date purchased _____
Discontinued 1998, 11" tall
Market value: $19.95, paid $_____

☐ **AUGUST**
#1958
Issued 1996, Date purchased _____
Discontinued 1998, 11" tall
Market value: $19.95, paid $_____

☐ **SEPTEMBER**
#1959
Issued 1996, Date purchased _____
Discontinued 1998, 11" tall
Market value: $19.95, paid $_____

☐ **OCTOBER**
#1960
Issued 1996, Date purchased _____
Discontinued 1998, 11" tall
Market value: $19.95, paid $_____

☐ **NOVEMBER**
#1961
Issued 1996, Date purchased _____
Discontinued 1998, 11" tall
Market value: $19.95, paid $_____

☐ **DECEMBER**
#1962
Issued 1996, Date purchased _____
Discontinued 1998, 11" tall
Market value: $19.95, paid $_____

CAREER SERIES

POSTAL WORKER
#1310
Issued July 1999, Date purchased _____
Current, 12" tall
Market value: $31.00, paid $_____

Postal Worker wears a blue pair of slacks and white blouse
with a red tie. She also has a blue jacket and a blue hat with
red and white stripes. She is carrying a brown bag with the
word "MAIL" written in white.

TEACHER
#1414
Issued July 1997, Date purchased _____
Current, 12" tall
Market value: $31.00, paid $_____

Teacher is the first edition in the Career Series. She is dressed
in a denim jumper with a light blue blouse. On the front of the
blouse is an apple. She is wearing a pair of eyeglasses. The
dress can be personalized.

AFRICAN-AMERICAN TEACHER
#1414A
Issued 1997, Date purchased _____
Current, 12" tall
Market value: $31.00, paid $_____

Teacher is the first edition in the Career Series. She is dressed
in a denim jumper with a light blue blouse. On the front of
the blouse is an apple. She is wearing a pair of eyeglasses.
The dress can be personalized.

NURSE
#1415
Issued 1998, Date purchased _____
Current, 12" tall
Market value: $31.00, paid $_____

Nurse is the second edition in the Career Series. She is dressed in her white nurse's uniform. On her head is a little white cap. She is also wearing white shoes and white stockings. The lab coat can be personalized.

CHEF
#1454
Issued January 1999, Date purchased _____
Current, 12" tall
Market value: $31.00, paid $_____

Chef is the third edition the Career Series. She is wearing a white chef coat with a plaid dress under it. She has white stockings and black shoes. On her head is a white chef's hat which can be personalized.

COLEENIA WITH CLOWN
#1027
Issued 1991, Date purchased _____
Limited two years, 16" tall
Market value: $350.00 – 375.00, paid $ _____

Coleenia is wearing a long white dress and a pink bow in her long blond hair. She is carrying a clown doll.

CHAPEL FAN DOLL – CAUCASIAN
#1039
Issued 1992, Date purchased _____
Current, 16" tall
Market value: $50.00, paid $ _____

CHAPEL FAN DOLL – AFRICAN-AMERICAN
#1040
Issued 1992, Date purchased _____
Current, 16" tall
Market value: $50.00, paid $ _____

Each of these dolls is dressed in a beige print pinafore with beige eyelet lace, layered to accent her pantaloon and sleeves. The doll on the right has pigtails tied with green bows. They are both carrying fans that read "I'm a Precious Moments Fan."

DANIEL THE SHEPHERD
#1055
Issued 1994, Date purchased _____
Current, 16" tall
Market value: $40.00, paid $_____

Daniel The Shepherd is clothed in a dark green shepherd's coat over a brown gown. His woven sash is multicolored and he has brown molded sandals. Only available at "Shepherd of the Hills" near Branson, Missouri.

CHAPEL INDIAN DOLL
#1058
Issued 1994, Date purchased _____
Limited 200, 16" tall
Market value: $475.00 – 500.00, paid $_____

This Indian squaw is dressed in a light gray leather dress with leather strips threaded through turquoise, silver, and maroon beads. On her head is a turquoise feather.

BESS WITH MAP
#1075
Issued 1993, Date purchased _____
Current, 16" tall
Market value: $35.00, paid $_____

Bess's peach print dress is accented with eyelet lace. She has matching bows in her hair. The map in her hands shows the way to the Precious Moments Chapel in Carthage, Missouri.

MAUREEN
#1084
Issued 1997, Date purchased _____
Current, 16" tall
Market value: $50.00, paid $_____

Maureen is dressed in a lovely, white satin gown with hearts on the skirt. The buttons on the front of the bodice and cuffs are heart-shaped.

PM COLLECTOR
#1095
Issued 1995, Date purchased _____
Current, 16" tall
Market value: $40.00, paid $_____

The PM Collector doll sports a comfortable pair of blue jeans and a pink sweatshirt that has two angels on a cloud in the middle sending a message, "Love Goes on Forever." She has a yellow hat that adorns her curly brunette hair.

COLETTE
#1097
Issued 1996, Date purchased _____
Current, 16" tall
Market value: $45.00, paid $_____

Colette displays a rainbow of pastel colors of pink, yellow, green, and blue with a big bow on the front of her dress. She is wearing gold shoes with bows on the top.

These Fourth of July Dolls have red, white, and blue dresses with white stars on them. The little girls have red and white ribbons in their hair. The dolls came in three hair color versions: red, brown, and blond.

FOURTH OF JULY DOLL
#1056
Issued 1997, Date purchased _____
Limited 2,016, 9" tall
Market value: $49.95, paid $ _____

FOURTH OF JULY DOLL
#1105
Issued 1997, Date purchased _____
Limited 2,016, 7" tall
Market value: $49.95, paid $_____

TIFFANY BROOKE
#1121
Issued 2001, Date purchased _____
Current, 16" tall
Market value: $55.00, paid $_____

Tiffany Brooke is lovely in her red satin dress with white lace sleeves and trim. Each tier of the dress is trimmed in gold braid. Her red satin hair bow matches her satin slippers.

DUSTIN
#1497
Issued 1995, Date purchased _____
Limited 2,000, 12" tall
Market value: $25.00, paid $ _____

DUSTIN
#1103
Issued 1995, Date purchased _____
Limited 750, 16" tall
Market value: $30.00, paid $ _____

Dustin is dressed in a Victorian era coat, knickers, and hat fashioned from white on white rocade trimmed in white satin ribbon and pearl buttons.

LINDSAY
#1102
Issued 1995, Date purchased _____
Limited 750, 16" tall
Market value: $30.00, paid $ _____

LINDSAY
#1496
Issued 1995, Date purchased _____
Limited 2,000, 12" tall
Market value: $25.00, paid $ _____

Lindsay is clad in a white Victorian laced dress with a matching white bonnet. She has long brown curly hair.

MAGGIE ZENE
#1131
Issued 1998, Date purchased _____
1 year production, 16" tall
Market value: $100.00 – 150.00, paid $ _____

Maggie Zene is dressed in a newsprint style dress with red ribbons and lace trim. She has pretty short black hair with little red ribbons. Sam Butcher designed her exclusively for *Chapel Bell* subscribers.

TIMMY ANGEL WITH CAKE
#1139
Issued 1999, Date purchased _____
Limited 500, 16" tall
Market value: $150.00 – 175.00, paid $ _____

Timmy was made to celebrate the Precious Moments Chapel's 10th anniversary. He is wearing a blue angelic gown with a halo on his head and is carrying a birthday cake.

EVELYN
#1146
Issued 1999, Date purchased _____
Limited 750, 16" tall
Market value: $250.00 – 275.00, paid $ _____

Sam designed this pretty little doll in honor of his mother. She is wearing an elegant dress of cascade lace ruffles with pink accents, a wrist chain, and an ankle bracelet. Each doll came hand signed by Sam Butcher.

SAMMY FROM SUGAR TOWN
#1371
Issued 1998, Date purchased _____
Limited 1,000, 12" tall
Market value: $75.00 – 100.00, paid $ _____

Sammy is dressed in a pastel green jacket with a lavender scarf around his neck. He is also wearing lavender mittens, a lavender cap, and a black pair of slacks.

These darling little mermaids have attractive, colorful fins.
Each doll comes with blond, brown, or black hair.

☐ **MERMAID – GREEN**
#1580
Issued 2000, Date purchased _____
Current, 10" tall
Market value: $29.95, paid $_____

☐ **MERMAID – YELLOW**
#1581
Issued 2000, Date purchased _____
Current, 10" tall
Market value: $29.95, paid $_____

☐ **MERMAID – BLUE**
#1582
Issued 2000, Date purchased_____
Current, 10" tall
Market value: $29.95, paid $_____

☐ **MERMAID – PINK**
#1583
Issued 2000, Date purchased_____
Current, 10" tall
Market value: $29.95, paid $_____

☐ **SAFARI SUE**
#1693
Issued 2000, Date purchased _____
Limited 1,200, 7" tall
Market value: $100.00 – 125.00, paid $_____

This doll was part of the registration package at the Chapel's
6th Annual Licensee Event and Collector's Weekend in 2000.
She is dressed in a leopard print safari outfit with a matching
leopard hat and pair of red knickers. She has curly blond hair.

FAITH (BLUE)
#1694
Issued 2000, Date purchased _____
Current, 4" tall
Market value: $7.00, paid $_____

Faith is a pretty angel wearing a light blue gown and carrying a little cross. She has long brown hair with a halo in it.

LOVE (PINK)
#1695
Issued 2000, Date purchased _____
Current, 4" tall
Market value: $7.00, paid $_____

Love wears a pink gown and carries a little heart. She has long blond hair with a white bow in it.

HOPE (PURPLE)
#1696
Issued 2000, Date purchased _____
Current, 4" tall
Market value: $7.00, paid $_____

Hope's gown is lavender and light green and she has long dark hair with a halo on her head. She carries a little star.

JOY (GREEN)
#1697
Issued 2000, Date purchased _____
Current, 4" tall
Market value: $7.00, paid $_____

Joy features a white gown with a peach shawl. She holds a little yellow flower and has long brown hair with a teal ribbon in it.

☐ **TAMMY**
#1699
Issued 2000, Date purchased _____
Current, 7" tall
Market value: $13.00, paid $ _____

☐ **TIMMY**
#1698
Issued 2000, Date purchased _____
Current, 7" tall
Market value: $13.00, paid $ _____

Tammy and Timmy angels have golden blond hair and are wearing white gowns. They have golden halos on their heads and wings on their backs.

☐ **JAMIE**
#9001E
Issued 1994, Date purchased _____
1 year production, 16" tall
Market value: $250.00 – 275.00, paid $ _____

Jamie has curly brown hair and is wearing a cute yellow bunny outfit with a white ribbon hanging from his neck.

☐ **BLOND CASEY**
#1022A
Issued 1991, Date purchased _____
Limited 200, 16" tall
Market value: $250.00 – 275.00, paid $ _____

Casey is ready for a game of baseball. Dressed in a blue and white striped uniform with red accents and baseball cap, he carries his baseball glove. He is similar to #1022 Casey (page 93) but has blond hair.

CHILDREN OF THE BIBLE

☐ **DAVID**
#1568
Issued 1999, Date purchased _____
Suspended January 2001, 12" tall
Market value: $21.00, paid $_____

David is the first edition in the "Children of the Bible" series. With curly blond hair and a bandana around it, he is dressed in red, brown, and gray ancient clothing. He is carrying a leather bag and wearing sandals.

☐ **DANIEL & LION**
#1569
Issued 1999, Date purchased _____
Suspended January 2001, 12" tall
Market value: $21.00, paid $_____

This doll set is also part of the "Children of the Bible" series. Daniel, accompanied by his lion friend, wears a white top with a rope around his waist. He also has brown pants and a pair of sandals on his feet.

CHILDREN OF THE WORLD

☐ **CARLA – UNITED STATES**
#1501
Issued 1989, Date purchased _____
Retired 1997, 9" tall
Market value: $55.00 – 65.00, paid $_____

Carla is dressed in a two-tone, mauve dress with a black ribbon around her waist and black bow at her neckline. She has pink ribbons in her hair.

MAZIE – AFRICAN-AMERICAN
#1502
Issued 1989, Date purchased _____
Retired 1994, 9" tall
Market value: $65.00 – 75.00, paid $ _____

Mazie is wearing a tan and flowered print dress with a blue hemline. She has a black ribbon around her dress and black ribbon at the neckline, as well as a blue ribbon in her hair.

SHANNON – IRELAND
#1503
Issued 1989, Date purchased _____
Retired 1998, 9" tall
Market value: $55.00 – 65.00, paid $ _____

Shannon is dressed in a green and white polka dot dress and is wearing a white blouse. She has pretty red hair with a green ribbon in it.

CORY – PHILIPPINES
#1504
Issued 1989, Date purchased _____
Retired 1992, 9" tall
Market value: $55.00 – 65.00, paid $ _____

Cory has a yellow and floral native dress. In her pretty black hair on the left side of her head is a yellow flower.

SHONNIE – NATIVE AMERICAN
#1505
Issued 1989, Date purchased _____
Retired 1991, 9" tall
Market value: $400.00 – 500.00, paid $ _____

Shonnie is dressed in a two-piece light tan outfit with red, yellow, white, and black bands of beads around the neckline, waistline, head, and hemline. Her hair is fixed in long black ponytails.

MISU – JAPAN
#1506
Issued 1989, Date purchased _____
Retired 1995, 9" tall
Market value: $150.00 – 175.00, paid $ _____

Misu is dressed in a pink kimono with burgundy trim. She has short black hair put up into a small tail with a burgundy ribbon.

MARIA – SPAIN
#1507
Issued 1990, Date purchased _____
Retired 2001, 9" tall
Market value: $55.00 – 65.00, paid $ _____

Maria is a pretty doll with dark eyes and hair that wears a festive looking long, red dress of ruffles with a small border of black lace showing on the four tiers.

GRETEL – SWEDEN
#1508
Issued 1990, Date purchased _____
Retired 1999, 9" tall
Market value: $55.00 – 65.00, paid $ _____

Gretel has blond hair and blue eyes and is dressed in a white blouse and black skirt with a pink satin apron on top.

KARI – NETHERLANDS
#1509
Issued 1989, Date purchased _____
Retired 1998, 9" tall
Market value: $55.00 – 65.00, paid $ _____

Kari is a cute little doll with blond braids, blue eyes, a white Dutch hat, and black shoes that resemble authentic wooden Dutch shoes.

SULU – ALASKA (BROWN)
#1510
Issued 1990, Date purchased _____
Retired 1996, 9" tall
Market value: $60.00 – 70.00, paid $ _____

Sulu is wearing brown fur-like pants, coat, and hat. She has beautiful dark skin and long black hair that is parted in the middle.

SULU – ALASKA (WHITE)
#1510A
Issued 1996, Date purchased _____
Current, 9" tall
Market value: $21.00, paid $_____

Sulu is wearing white fur-like pants and coat with brown trim, as well as a brown fur-like hat. This one still has the original beautiful dark skin and long black hair, but instead of it being parted in the middle, she grew bangs.

IVAN – RUSSIA
#1511
Issued 1990, Date purchased _____
Retired 1995, 9" tall
Market value: $100.00 – 125.00, paid $ _____

This adorable little Russian boy has sweet blue eyes and blond hair and wears a black jacket, black boots, a black fur-like hat, and red pants.

GRETCHEN – GERMANY
#1512
Issued 1990, Date purchased _____
Retired 1994, 9" tall
Market value: $50.00 – 100.00, paid $ _____

Gretchen has blond braids, blue eyes, and an authentic looking German outfit, complete with hat and apron. When Gretchen was first issued, the bottom border on her apron was yellow and she had a white feather in her hat.

TAYA – INDIA
#1513
Issued 1995, Date purchased _____
Retired 2001, 9" tall
Market value: $55.00 – 65.00, paid $ _____

Taya has beautiful dark skin, dark hair pulled back in a ponytail, dark eyes, light blue satin garments, and wears a red dot on her forehead.

ANGELINA – ITALY
#1514
Issued 1995, Date purchased _____
Retired 2001, 9" tall
Market value: $55.00 – 65.00, paid $ _____

Angelina has sweet green eyes, brown hair that has been braided and pulled up under her white lacy head covering, and wears a red skirt, white blouse with matching apron, a green floral shawl, green beaded necklace, and brown sandals.

HANS – DENMARK
#1515
Issued 1995, Date purchased _____
Retired 1999, 9" tall
Market value: $55.00 – 65.00, paid $ _____

Hans is dressed in his native costume, a blue/gray jacket and black shoes. He is also wearing a black hat complete with a white feather.

SOPHIE – POLAND
#1516
Issued 1995, Date purchased _____
Current, 9" tall
Market value: $21.00, paid $_____

Sophie has dark blond hair with a lovely floral wreath atop, brown eyes, and wears a black floral skirt with a matching vest and apron over a white blouse.

MORNING GLORY – NATIVE AMERICAN
#1517
Issued 1995, Date purchased _____
Current, 9" tall
Market value: $21.00, paid $_____

Morning Glory has beautiful dark skin and eyes, dark cropped hair with a headband complete with a feather, and wears an authentic looking tan smock.

PUALANI – HAWAII
#1518
Issued 1995, Date purchased _____
1 year production, 9" tall
Market value: $21.00, paid $_____

Pualani has dark eyes, long black hair with a yellow flower that matches her lei of red flowers. She also wears a festive long grass skirt. This doll was limited to one-year production.

FREYA – DENMARK
#1519
Issued 1996, Date purchased _____
Retired 2001, 9" tall
Market value: $55.00 – 65.00, paid $_____

Freya wears a dark, rose-colored dress with a matching calico print apron and collar and a dark green bonnet. She has long brown hair with sweet long curls and bright green eyes.

OLLIE – NORWAY
#1523
Issued 1996, Date purchased _____
Current, 9" tall
Market value: $21.00, paid $_____

Ollie has pretty long blond hair and wears an authentic looking Norwegian outfit complete with red hat, and a red matching apron.

AISHA – AFRICA
#1524
Issued 1996, Date purchased _____
Current, 9" tall
Market value: $21.00, paid $_____

Aisha has beautiful golden, dark skin and short, dark, curly hair that's covered in a bright scarf that matches her bright striped wrapped dress. She wears cute little black sandals and sweet gold hoop earrings.

MEI MEI – CHINA
#1525
Issued 1997, Date purchased _____
Current, 9" tall
Market value: $21.00, paid $_____

Mei Mei has sweet dark eyes, black cropped hair with a pink flower in it and wears a precious bright pink satin pantsuit.

YOIM – KOREA
#1526
Issued 1997, Date purchased _____
Current, 9" tall
Market value: $21.00, paid $_____

Yoim has bright dark eyes and straight long black hair with a red flower that matches her long authentic looking red dress with adorning golden print and bright stripes.

ALOHALANI – HAWAII
#1527
Issued 1996, Date purchased _____
Current, 9" tall
Market value: $100.00, paid $_____

Alohalani has pretty dark eyes and long black hair with a wreath of bright pink flowers on top. She wears a festive long light pink gown with bright pink ruffles and a pink lei.

KEIKI-LANI – HAWAII
#1528
Issued 1996, Date purchased _____
Current, 9" tall
Market value: $100.00, paid $_____

Keiki-Lani has pretty dark eyes, long black hair, and a wreath of flowers on her head. She wears a festive long blue flowered gown with purple ruffles.

ALLISON – UNITED STATES
#1529
Issued 1996, Date purchased _____
Current, 9" tall
Market value: $21.00, paid $_____

Allison has a blue denim jumper-dress with a red and white checkered blouse underneath. Her light blond hair is pulled back in a ponytail with a blue bow.

MARISOL – PUERTO RICO
#1530
Issued 1998, Date purchased _____
Current, 9" tall
Market value: $69.95, paid $_____

Marisol looks lovely with her dark ponytail hair, authentic looking outfit, pretty beaded necklace, and hoop earrings.

NAHKEEN – ALASKA
#1531
Issued 1998, Date purchased _____
Current, 9" tall
Market value: $69.95, paid $_____

Nahkeen looks adorable with her dark hair and eyes. She is dressed in an authentic tan outfit with a pretty multicolored shawl. She is wearing moccasins on her feet.

KATRINA – DUTCH
#1532
Issued 1998, Date purchased _____
Current, 9" tall
Market value: $21.00, paid $_____

Katrina has long blond braids, bright blue eyes, and wears a pretty cornflower blue dress, white Dutch hat adorned with lace, and sweet little Dutch shoes.

PIETER – DUTCH
#1533
Issued 1998, Date purchased _____
Current, 9" tall
Market value: $21.00, paid $_____

Pieter is dressed in a blue cornflower suit with matching blue hat. He is wearing a pair of little Dutch shoes. He is the twin brother to Katrina.

JUAN – MEXICO
#1534
Issued 1998, Date purchased _____
Current, 9" tall
Market value: $21.00, paid $_____

Juan has handsome dark skin, hair, and eyes and wears an authentic looking Mexican outfit complete with sandals and a big sombrero.

ISIS – EGYPT
#1535
Issued 1998, Date purchased _____
Suspended 2001, 9" tall
Market value: $60.00 – 70.00, paid $ _____

Isis has sweet dark eyes, black cropped hair and a bright golden metallic Egyptian outfit with matching headress. She is also wearing a pair of Egyptian sandals.

CAITLYN – IRELAND
#1536
Issued 1999, Date purchased _____
Current, 9" tall
Market value: $21.00, paid $_____

Caitlyn is a pretty little doll with red hair that wears a green print dress and a big gray wool coat with a hood. Her hair is done in a ponytail.

KYOTO – JAPAN
#1537
Issued 2000, Date purchased _____
Current, 9" tall
Market value: $21.00, paid $_____

Kyoto, with dark hair and eyes, wears a lavender Japanese kimono and has a flower in her hair. On her feet she has a pair of Japanese wooden shoes.

MALCOLM – SCOTLAND
#1538
Issued 1999, Date purchased _____
Current, 9" tall
Market value: $21.00, paid $_____

Malcolm is a handsome boy doll with blond hair that wears a red, green, and white plaid kilt, white shirt with a tie, green jacket, and a green hat.

SUNISA – THAILAND
#1539
Issued 1999, Date purchased _____
Current, 9" tall
Market value: $21.00, paid $_____

Sunisa is an attractive doll with dark eyes and long black hair pulled back in a long braid down her back. She is wearing a bright and festive looking garment made of shiny bright blue satin and gold print. She is also wearing an ornate golden headdress, a satin cape, and no shoes.

SOUHAILA – LEBANON
#1540
Issued 1999, Date purchased _____
Current, 9" tall
Market value: $21.00, paid $_____

Souhaila is a sweet doll with dark eyes and hair wearing a light blue checkered dress with yellow and pink accent striping. She is also wearing a white scarf on her head.

SYLVIE – CANADA
#1541
Issued 2000, Date purchased _____
Current, 9" tall
Market value: $21.00, paid $_____

Sylvie is an adorable little doll with dark blond hair worn in braids and blue eyes. She is wearing a warm outfit that is decorated with a red maple leaf print.

CATHERINE – ENGLAND
#1542
Issued 2000, Date purchased _____
Current, 9" tall
Market value: $21.00, paid $_____

Catherine has dark blond hair and blue eyes. She is wearing a dark blue plaid skirt, blue jacket, and hat.

LUMEN – PHILIPPINES
#1543
Issued 2000, Date purchased _____
Current, 9" tall
Market value: $21.00, paid $_____

Lumen, a pretty little doll with dark hair and eyes, is wearing a red satin skirt with black lace overlay, a white blouse, and a bun in her hair.

SACHIKO – HAWAII
#1544
Issued 2000, Date purchased _____
Current, 9" tall
Market value: $59.00, paid $_____

Sachiko has dark hair and eyes and a gorgeous red gown with a gold colored belt around her waist. She has her hair pulled up with flowers. Sachiko is a Cathedral Gift Shop Exclusive in Hawaii.

KYLENE – AUSTRALIA
#1545
Issued 2001, Date purchased _____
Current, 9" tall
Market value: $21.00, paid $_____

Kylene is clad in an Aussie outfit of tan and green with a matching hat. She has dark blond hair and blue eyes.

LILY – SINGAPORE
#1546
Issued 2001, Date purchased _____
Current, 9" tall
Market value: $21.00, paid $_____

Lily has dark eyes and black hair and wears a bright, festive looking floral garment with gold trim.

JACQUE – FRANCE
#1547
Issued 2001, Date purchased _____
Current, 9" tall
Market value: $21.00, paid $_____

Jacque is a handsome little doll wearing a black beret and a bright red jacket. He has on a black and white striped shirt and black slacks.

KENISHA – JAMAICA
#1548
Issued 2001, Date purchased _____
Current, 9" tall
Market value: $21.00, paid $_____

Kenisha is a pretty doll with dark eyes and black hair. She is wearing a bright, festive looking garment and carries fruit on her headscarf.

LEILANI – HAWAII
#1549

Issued 2001, Date purchased _____
Current, 9" tall
Market value: $21.00, paid $_____

Leilani is a pretty little doll with long dark hair and dark eyes.
She is wearing a pastel colored top with a light blue hula skirt.
She is barefoot.

LEIKELALANI – HAWAII
#1550

Issued 2001, Date purchased _____
Current, 9" tall
Market value: $25.00, paid $_____

Leikelalani also has long dark hair and dark eyes. She is wearing
two Hawaiian leis and a light green hula skirt. She has no shoes
on her feet. This doll is a Food Pantry Exclusive in Hawaii.

XSING – VIETNAM
#4130

Issued August 2002, Date purchased _____
Current, 9" tall
Market value: $21.00, paid $_____

Xsing is dressed in a native Vietnamese red gown with a large
straw hat on her head. She has red sandals on her feet and
long black hair.

FIONA – IRELAND
#4131

Issued August 2002, Date purchased _____
Current, 9" tall
Market value: $21.00, paid $_____

Fiona is dressed in a green printed skirt with white lace
trim and has a green vest with a white blouse. She has
beautiful curly blond hair with green flower accents.

SUZIE – SWITZERLAND
#4132
Issued October 2002, Date purchased _____
Current, 9" tall
Market value: $21.00, paid $ _____

Suzie models a cute blue print dress with a white and pink apron. She has blond hair with pink flower accents.

JUANITA – MEXICO
#4133
Issued August 2002, Date purchased _____
Current, 9" tall
Market value: $21.00, paid $ _____

Juanita has long black hair made into ponytails. She is wearing a traditional Mexican outfit and a large straw sombrero.

INDIRA – INDIA
#4134
Issued October 2002, Date purchased _____
Current, 9" tall
Market value: $21.00, paid $_____

Indira has long black hair with a lavender print shawl on her head. She is wearing a traditional Indian outfit in lavender with flower accents.

MARGUERITE – FRANCE
#4135
Issued August 2002, Date purchased _____
Current, 9" tall
Market value: $21.00, paid $_____

Marguerite is a cute French girl with short blond hair. She is wearing a pretty pink and white lace dress with a matching hat.

CHRISTMAS CLASSIC DOLL COLLECTION

□ MRS. SANTA
#1206
Issued 1998, Date purchased _____
Limited 5,000, 16" tall
Market value: $79.95, paid $ _____

Mrs. Santa has white hair and wears glasses, emerald colored earrings, a red cap, and a festive red dress with a white satin apron and carries a big wrapped present in her hands.

□ MR. SANTA
#1205
Issued 1998, Date purchased _____
Limited 5,000, 16" tall
Market value: $79.95, paid $ _____

Mr. Santa has white hair and a white beard and wears glasses, a red hat, red vest, green velvet pants, and black boots. He carries a big burlap sack full of toys on his back.

□ CANDY
#1208
Issued 1999, Date purchased _____
Limited 5,000, 16" tall
Market value: $80.00 – 100.00, paid $ _____

Candy is wearing a festive red and white satin dress with candy cane print trim, red shoes, red bow, and a red crushed velvet coat complete with hood. She has light blond hair and brown eyes.

STEPHANIE
#1211
Issued 1994, Date purchased _____
Limited 7,500, 16" tall
Market value: $250.00 – 275.00, paid $_____

Stephanie's hair is up in two pretty ponytails that are fastened with red ribbons. She is wearing a delightful red and green plaid dress full of ruffles and trimmed with white lace, diamond-like earrings, and a beautiful green velvet coat complete with a white fur trimmed hood and muff.

MARCY
#1207
Issued 1993, Date purchased _____
Limited 6,000, 16" tall
Market value: $350.00 – 375.00, paid $_____

Marcy is wearing a fancy green velvet dress trimmed with red plaid material and lace and shiny black patent shoes. She also wears a green velvet cape and carries a purse.

JANNA
#1215
Issued 1997, Date purchased _____
Limited 5,000, 16" tall
Market value: $100.00 – 125.00, paid $_____

Janna is clothed in a white satin gown trimmed with silver and faux white fur. A matching hat tops her head and she wears pretty white boots.

☐ **GLORIA**
 #1217
Issued 1995, Date purchased _____
Limited 7,500, 16" tall
Market value: $150.00 – 175.00, paid $ _____

Gloria is wearing a white satin gown with gold and pearl trim and white satin ballet shoes. She has gorgeous golden hair in spiral curls and big blue eyes.

☐ **STAR**
 #1220
Issued 1996, Date purchased _____
Limited 5,000, 16" tall
Market value: $140.00 – 150.00, paid $_____

Star has beautiful straight golden hair and green eyes. She is wearing fur-lined boots and mittens, a dark green corduroy dress trimmed with green satin, and a burgundy coat trimmed in dark green. Star wears diamond-like earrings and carries sheet music for caroling.

☐ **KRISTINA KRINGLE**
 #1151
Issued October 2002, Date purchased _____
Current, 16" tall
Market value: $30.00, paid $ _____

Kristina is ready for Christmas in her red velvet dress accented in white fluffy trim and hollies and a matching hat. She has long curly blond hair and comes with a matching red Christmas stocking.

GABRIELLE
#1150
Issued 2001, Date purchased _____
Current, 16" tall
Market value: $27.00, paid $ _____

Gabrielle is wearing a beautiful burgundy and hunter green velour dress with a wonderfully detailed stocking. Her hair is golden blond pulled into a single braid in the back, accented with holly leaves and a burgundy ribbon.

SANTA'S HELPER (GIRL)
#1344
Issued 2000, Date purchased _____
Current, 12" tall
Market value: $29.95, paid $_____

She is dressed in a white and red velvet dress with green elves' shoes. She is also wearing a green, red, and white polka dot elf's hat with a bell on the end and carries a teddy bear.

SANTA'S HELPER (BOY)
#1345
Issued 2000, Date purchased _____
Current, 12" tall
Market value: $29.95, paid $ _____

He is dressed in green pants and a white shirt, both trimmed at the sleeves in red and green. He also wears a red, white, and green vest and a red and green hat.

IT'S SNOW FUN WITHOUT YOU
#1366
Issued 2001, Date purchased _____
Current, 12" tall
Market value: $29.50, paid $_____

This snowwoman has long blond hair that is in ponytails. She is dressed in a fun snowman outfit with lavender and white polka-dotted mittens and lavender buttons. She also has a lavender and light blue scarf and matching hat. Her carrot nose is removable.

IT'S SNOW FUN WITHOUT YOU
#1367
Issued 2001, Date purchased _____
Current, 12" tall
Market value: $29.50, paid $_____

This snowwoman has long brown hair that is in ponytails. Like #1366, she, too, is dressed in a fun snowman outfit but this time with red and white polka dot mittens and tan buttons. She also has a red and green scarf and matching hat. Her nose is removable.

These cute little dolls are dressed in red and green Christmas outfits. The boy doll has a green hat. All three dolls are carrying sheet music.

REGINA
#1552
Issued 1996, Date purchased _____
Current, 9" tall
Market value: $21.00, paid $ _____

IAN
#1553
Issued 1996, Date purchased _____
Current, 9" tall
Market value: $21.00, paid $ _____

NATALIE
#1551
Issued 1996, Date purchased _____
Current, 9" tall
Market value: $21.00, paid $_____

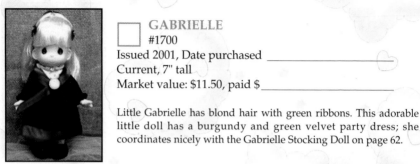

GABRIELLE
#1700
Issued 2001, Date purchased _____
Current, 7" tall
Market value: $11.50, paid $_____

Little Gabrielle has blond hair with green ribbons. This adorable little doll has a burgundy and green velvet party dress; she coordinates nicely with the Gabrielle Stocking Doll on page 62.

CHRISTY
#2001
Issued 1989, Date purchased _____
Retired 1998, 9" tall
Market value: $55.00 – 65.00, paid $_____

This pretty little tree topper is wearing a beautiful angelic white gown with gold trim. She has a halo on her head and on her back a pair of white and gold trimmed angel wings.

CHRISTY
#2001A
Issued 1998, Date purchased _____
Current, 9" tall
Market value: $25.00, paid $_____

This doll matches tree topper #2001, but her hair is pulled up with a gold ribbon.

CARRIE
#2002
Issued 1989, Date purchased _____
Suspended 1991, 9" tall
Market value: $75.00 – 85.00, paid $_____

Carrie is an African-American angel tree topper wearing a white angelic gown with gold trim. She has a gold halo on her head and a pair of white and gold trimmed wings on her back.

☐ **CHRISTIE**
#2003
Issued 1989, Date purchased _____
1 year production, 3" tall
Market value: $35.00 – 50.00, paid $ _____

This doll head is a Christmas ornament with a white collar that
has gold trim. Atop her head is an angel halo.

☐ **CARRIE**
#2004
Issued 1989, Date purchased _____ _____
1 year production, 3" tall
Market value: $35.00 – 50.00, paid $_____

This African-American angel head is a Christmas ornament
with a white collar that has gold trim. She has a halo on her
head.

☐ **TIMMY**
#2005
Issued 1991, Date purchased _____
Suspended 1994, 9" tall
Market value: $75.00 – 85.00, paid $_____

Timmy is a tree topper dressed in a white angelic gown
trimmed in gold. On his head is a gold halo.

☐ **HARMONY**
#2006
Issued 1995, Date purchased _____
Suspended 1996, 9" tall
Market value: $50.00 – 75.00, paid $ _____

Harmony wears a dark green gown trimmed in ecru lace. She is
carrying a gold foil gift box with golden stars. Her hair is up in
a bun with a green ribbon and she has angel wings on her back.
This doll is a tree topper.

☐ **PEACE**
#2007
Issued 1995, Date purchased _____
Suspended 1996, 9" tall
Market value: $50.00 – 75.00, paid $ _____

Peace is a tree topper dressed in a beautiful burgundy gown trimmed in gold. She is carrying a gold foil box with wine colored roses. She has her hair up in a bun with a red ribbon to match her dress. On her back are angel wings.

☐ **JOY**
#2008
Issued 1995, Date purchased _____
Suspended 1996, 9" tall
Market value: $50.00 – 75.00, paid $ _____

Joy is dressed in a white angelic gown with gold trim. She is carrying a gold foil box. She has golden wings on her back. This doll is a tree topper.

☐ **GOLD ANGEL**
#2009
Issued 1995, Date purchased _____
Suspended 2001, 7" tall
Market value: $25.00 – 50.00, paid $ _____

This little angel is an ornament. He is dressed in a white angelic gown with gold trim. He has a gold halo on his head.

☐ **SILVER ANGEL**
#2010
Issued 1995, Date purchased _____
Suspended 1998, 7" tall
Market value: $25.00 – 50.00, paid $ _____

This Christmas angel is an ornament dressed in a silver angelic gown. He has a silver halo on his head.

ANGELICA
#2011
Issued 1996, Date purchased _____
Limited 5,000, 12" tall
Market value: $75.00 – 100.00, paid $ _____

Angelica is dressed in a beautiful white satin gown with over-sized tulle. She has a gold beaded halo on her head and a gold beaded necklace around her neck. This doll is a tree topper.

CELESTE
#2015
Issued 1997, Date purchased _____
Limited 5,000, 12" tall
Market value: $75.00 – 100.00, paid $ _____

Celeste is a tree topper dressed in a white satin angelic gown. She has long blond curly hair.

GABRIELLE
#2018
Issued 1998, Date purchased _____
Limited 5,000, 12" tall
Market value: $39.95, paid $ _____

Gabrielle is dressed in a white satin angelic gown trimmed in gold. She has large golden wings on her back. This doll is a tree topper.

GOLD FLYING ANGEL II
#2019
Issued 1998, Date purchased _____
Current, 7" tall
Market value: $19.95, paid $_____

This flying angel is a Christmas ornament dressed in a white satin gown, trimmed in gold. She has long curly blond hair.

☐ **KIMBERLY**
#2020
Issued 1999, Date purchased _____
Limited 5,000, 12" tall
Market value: $39.95, paid $_____

Kimberly is dressed in a beautiful white gown with large heavenly wings on her back. She has long blond curly hair.

☐ **CELESTIAL**
#2022
Issued 2001, Date purchased _____
Current, 9" tall
Market value: $31.00, paid $_____

Celestial is a tree topper in a gorgeous golden dress with real feather wings on her back. This doll's ribbon banner can be personalized.

☐ **SAMMY CLAUS**
#4215
Issued 2001, Date purchased _____
Current, 12" tall
Market value: $29.50, paid $_____

This special doll was created by Sam Butcher himself. Each doll's pallet has been personally signed by him. Proceeds from the sale of the dolls benefit his Overseas foundation.

JOY TREE TOPPER
#2023
Issued October 2002, Date purchased _____
Current, 12" tall
Market value: $38.00, paid $_____

Beautiful Joy angel tree topper is dressed in a white angelic gown and has gold wings on her back. She has long straight blond hair. She comes with a banner that can be personalized.

PEACE TREE TOPPER
#2024
Issued October 2002, Date purchased _____
Current, 12" tall
Market value: $38.00, paid $_____

Peace angel tree topper is dressed in a red and white angelic gown and has white wings on her back. She has long curly blond hair. She comes with a banner that can be personalized.

HARMONY TREE TOPPER
#2025
Issued October 2002, Date purchased _____
Current, 12" tall
Market value: $38.00, paid $_____

Harmony tree topper is dressed in a white and gold angelic gown and has gold wing on her back. She has long curly blond hair. She comes with a banner that can be persoonalized.

CLASSIC COLLECTION

The "classic" dolls were created with the serious doll collector in mind. These dolls are very detailed. Many wear jewel earrings, patent leather shoes, velvet, satin, and lace.

☐ **ERICH**
#1065
Issued 1994, Date purchased _____
Limited 5,000, 16" tall
Market value: $175.00 – 200.00,
paid $ _____

Erich is dressed in a pair of brown knickers and red top with a matching red beret. He has leather-like shoes.

☐ **EMMA**
#1064
Issued 1994, Date purchased _____
Limited 5,000, 16" tall
Market value: $175.00 – 200.00,
paid $ _____

Emma is waring a patchwork skirt and a velvet tapestry vest. On her head is a crown of roses. She was the first doll with leather-like shoes.

☐ **PRINCESS MELODY**
#1200
Issued 1992, Date purchased _____
Limited 7,500, 16" tall
Market value: $500.00 – 525.00, paid $ _____

Princess Melody has long curly blond hair and wears an ornate pink and white satin dress that is trimmed with gold, pearls, and lace, a matching pink cape, and a jeweled tiara.

MELINDA
#1201
Issued 1992, Date purchased _____
Limited 7,000, 16" tall
Market value: $350.00 – 375.00, paid $ _____

Melinda is wearing a long light blue gown trimmed with white lace and has a matching bow in her hair. She has long wavy blond hair and blue eyes and wears pearl-like earrings and a ring. Melinda was named after Sam Butcher's daughter-in-law.

ANDREAH
#1202
Issued 1993, Date purchased _____
Limited 4,000, 16 " tall
Market value: $150.00 – 175.00, paid $ _____

Andreah has dark brown hair and eyes and is wearing a pretty pink satin gown trimmed in antique lace and a matching cap. Her collar is decorated with an oval pink cameo rose.

PAIGE WITH SCOTTY DOG
#1203
Issued 2002, Date purchased _____
Limited 2,500, 16" tall
Market value: $50.00, paid $_____

Paige is fashonable in her red plaid jumper with white blouse underneath her red coat. She has long curly dark blond hair, green eyes, and is wearing a red hat and gold colored stud earrings. She comes with her favorite black Scotty dog.

☐ **BRIDGET**
#1210
Issued 1994, Date purchased _____
Limited 7,500, 16" tall
Market value: $200.00 – 225.00, paid $_____

Bridget has long red curly hair and bright green eyes. She is wearing a blue and green wool plaid skirt, white blouse with a golden shamrock at the collar, and a white Irish sweater with matching stocking cap and sweater leggings. Bridget carries a white basket filled with shamrocks.

☐ **MIAKOTA**
#1213
Issued 1995, Date purchased _____
Limited 7,500, 16" tall
Market value: $200.00 – 225.00, paid $ _____

Miakota is wearing genuine leather clothes, the Apache tribe's traditional garb. She has dark black hair at her shoulders and displays a pretty set of earrings.

☐ **HAPPY**
#1214
Issued 1995, Date purchased _____
Limited 7,500, 16" tall
Market value: $200.00 – 225.00, paid $ _____

Happy has bright red yarn hair, big blue eyes, and a red nose. He is wearing a colorful clown outfit made of bright blue, red, and shiny gold material and has jingle bells attached to his hat and shoes. He is holding a white mask that fits his face.

SPRING HOPE BRIDE
#1238
Issued 1999, Date purchased _____
Limited 2,500, 16" tall
Market value: $79.95, paid $_____

Hope Bride is lovely in her long satin gown trimmed with faux pearls and lace that has long puffy sleeves and a matching long train that attaches with pearl-like buttons in the back. She has her light brunette hair pulled up on her head with tiny curls dangling down the side and wears a pretty white veil.

CLASSIC GROOM
#1237
Issued 1999, Date purchased _____
Current, 16" tall
Market value: $54.95, paid $_____

This groom has blond hair that is neatly parted on the side and wears a black tuxedo with tails, a bow tie, and a top hat.

CLASSIC SUMMER JOY BRIDE
#1239
Issued 1999, Date purchased _____
Limited 2,500, 16" tall
Market value: $79.95, paid $_____

Joy Bride is a vision in her long satin gown trimmed with faux pearls and lace that has short puffy sleeves and a matching long train that attaches with pearl-like buttons in the back. Her long blond straight hair is down and she wears a pretty white veil.

THE LORD IS MY SHEPHERD
#1242
Issued 1999, Date purchased _____
Limited 2,500, 16" tall
Market value: $89.95, paid $_____

This doll is dressed in a pretty lavender gown and holds a little lamb. She has curly blond hair with lavender ribbons in it.

CINDERELLA
#1563
Issued 2001, Date purchased _____
Current, 9" tall
Market value: $21.00, paid $_____

Cinderella wears a shimmering light blue gown and looks like she's from a fairy tale. She has her beautiful blond hair put up with a pretty tiara. She has white gloves on her hands.

RAPUNZEL
#1564
Issued 1999, Date purchased _____
Current, 9" tall
Market value: $21.00, paid $_____

Rapunzel is wearing a lovely green pastel dress accented with pink rosettes. Her long blond hair is braided and also accented with rosettes.

SNOW WHITE
#1572
Issued 2001, Date purchased _____
Current, 9" tall
Market value: $21.00, paid $_____

Snow White has dark hair and eyes and is wearing a satin bright blue, yellow, red, and white gown. A red ribbon is in her hair.

FAMOUS WOMEN

AMELIA EARHART
#1584
Issued 2001, Date purchased _____
Current, 9" tall
Market value: $21.00, paid $_____

Amelia sports a complete green flight outfit with a brown
fur-like collar. Molded to the head are her green flight helmet
and goggles.

BETSY ROSS
#1585
Issued 2001, Date purchased _____
Current, 9" tall
Market value: $21.00, paid $_____

Betsy is dressed in an old-fashioned blue print dress with a
white apron. She wears a white bonnet on her head and is
carrying an American flag.

CALAMITY JANE
#1586
Issued 2001, Date purchased _____
Current, 9" tall
Market value: $21.00, paid $_____

Jane is dressed in a tan western outfit with cowgirl boots.
Atop her long brown hair sits a tan cowgirl hat.

EMILY DICKINSON
#1587
Issued 2001, Date purchased _____
Current, 9" tall
Market value: $21.00, paid $_____

Emily has black hair and wears a dark red dress. There is a card attached to the sleeve explaining who Emily Dickinson was and why she is famous.

POCAHONTAS
#1588
Issued 2001, Date purchased _____
Current, 9" tall
Market value: $21.00, paid $_____

Pocahontas is dressed in a tan leather Indian outfit. Her hair is done in pigtails with a beaded band around her head. On her feet is a pair of moccasins. She has a card explaining who she is.

FANNY CROSBY
#1589
Issued 2001, Date purchased _____
Current, 9" tall
Market value: $21.00, paid $_____

Fanny is wearing a calico print dress and her hair in two braids curled up and fastened at the sides with pink ribbons. She comes with a card explaining who she is.

MARTHA WASHINGTON
#1590
Issued 2002, Date purchased _____
Current, 9" tall
Market value: $21.00, paid $_____

Martha, the first "First Lady" of the United States, is dressed in an old-fashioned pink and cream dress. She has a cameo around her neck.

HELEN KELLER
#1591
Issued 2002, Date purchased _____
Current, 9" tall
Market value: $21.00, paid $_____

Helen comes clothed in a pretty cream colored dress with ruffles on the bottom. She has brown hair.

MARIAN ANDERSON
#1592
Issued 2002, Date purchased _____
Current, 9" tall
Market value: $21.00, paid $_____

Marian models a beautiful pink dress with white flowers. She worked to overcome racial barriers, eventually becoming the first African-American singer to appear at the Metropolitan Opera House.

FOUR SEASONS DOLL COLLECTION

BROOKE – SPRING
#1069
Issued 1995, Date purchased _____
Suspended 1998, 16" tall
Market value: $50.00 – 75.00, paid $ _____

Brooke has long blond hair and blue eyes, and wears a yellow print dress, matching hat, and a lightweight pink jacket. She is carrying a pale yellow picnic basket.

MEGAN – SUMMER
#1070
Issued 1995, Date purchased _____
Suspended 1998, 16" tall
Market value: $50.00 – 75.00, paid $ _____

Megan has long brunette hair and blue eyes and is wearing a pastel print jumpsuit, yellow sandals, and a big straw hat. She is carrying a yellow picnic basket.

ASHLEY – AUTUMN
#1071
Issued 1995, Date purchased _____
Suspended 1998, 16" tall
Market value: $50.00 – 75.00, paid $ _____

Ashley is dressed in lovely fall colors, from her reddish-brown hat to her tan floral print skirt. She has long dark blond hair that is braided on the sides and she carries a basket of grapes.

WHITNEY – WINTER
#1072
Issued 1995, Date purchased _____
Suspended 1998, 16" tall
Market value: $50.00 – 75.00, paid $ _____

Whitney is dressed in a festive dark green satin dress with golden trim and carries a gold colored basket of berries and pinecones. She has long strawberry-blond hair and blue eyes.

♥ Loving ♥ Caring ♥ Sharing ♥

FRIENDS ACROSS AMERICA COLLECTION

☐ **COASTAL**
  #1644
Issued September 1998, Date purchased _____
Current, 7" tall
Market value: $12.00, paid $ _____

Coastal is ready for a day at the beach with tan shorts and a pink blouse. She has a tan straw hat on her head. In her blond hair are pink ribbons. She is carrying a pail and shovel.

☐ **SOUTHWEST**
  #1645
Issued September 1998, Date purchased _____
Current, 7" tall
Market value: $12.00, paid $ _____

This little boy doll is dressed in blue coveralls and white shirt. He is wearing a tan cowboy hat and a red and white bandana around his neck. He is carrying a rope.

☐ **NORTHEAST**
  #1646
Issued September 1998, Date purchased _____
Current, 7" tall
Market value: $12.00, paid $ _____

Northeast is dressed in a pink and lavender snowsuit with white fur-like trim around the hood, sleeves, and pant legs. Around her neck is a pink and green scarf. She is carrying a pink cloth bag with a teddy bear in it.

☐ **MOUNTAIN**
  #1647
Issued September 1998, Date purchased _____
Current, 7" tall
Market value: $12.00, paid $ _____

Mountain has brown hair up in ponytails with bluish ribbons. She is wearing a brown pair of shorts and yellow sweater, with a black belt at the waistline. She has a green backpack, a water canteen, and a blue bandana around her neck.

MAGGIE
#1854
Issued 2002, Date purchased _____
Current, 7" tall
Market value: $13.00, paid $_____

Maggie wears a blue denim dress with a white blouse. She has a blue denim hat atop her blond ponytails. She is carrying a bushel of apples.

MICHAEL
#1855
Issued 2002, Date purchased _____
Current, 7" tall
Market value: $13.00, paid $_____

Michael is dressed in blue denim coveralls with a red and white plaid shirt and matching blue denim hat. He is carrying a bushel of apples.

PENELOPE
#1856
Issued 2002, Date purchased _____
Current, 7" tall
Market value: $13.00, paid $_____

Penelope has pretty brown hair, lavender ribbons, and a denim dress with a lavender and white blouse. She is carrying a bushel of apples.

☐ **POLLY**
   #1857
Issued 2002, Date purchased _____
Current, 7" tall
Market value: $13.00, paid $ _____

Polly's pigtails are blond with pink ribbons. She is wearing blue slacks with a pink and blue denim top and carrying a bushel of apples.

☐ **JENNIFER**
   #1858
Issued 2002, Date purchased _____
Current, 7" tall
Market value: $13.00, paid $ _____

Jennifer has brown hair with a yellow ribbon and is dressed in a blue denim and yellow dress. She is carrying a bushel of apples.

☐ **MAYA**
   #1859
Issued 2002, Date purchased _____
Current, 7" tall
Market value: $13.00, paid $ _____

Maya is an African-American doll dressed in a blue denim dress with lavender and white sleeves. She has pretty black hair with lavender ribbons. She is carrying a bushel of apples.

FRIENDS AND BUDDIES COLLECTION

☐ **BIANCA**
#1616
Issued 1998, Date purchased _____
Current, 7" tall
Market value: $19.95, paid $_____

Bianca's blond hair is pulled up with a green bow. She is wearing a blue and white checkered dress with white sleeves. She is carrying a green and white checkered bag.

☐ **RHEA**
#1617
Issued 1998, Date purchased _____
Current, 7" tall
Market value: $19.95, paid $_____

Rhea has blond hair with a pink and white checkered hat. She is wearing a pink and white jumper with white sleeves and carrying a yellow and white bag.

☐ **FIONA**
#1618
Issued 1998, Date purchased _____
Current, 7" tall
Market value: $19.95, paid $_____

Fiona has brown hair pulled into ponytails with yellow ribbons. She is dressed in a yellow and white checkered shorts set with white sleeves. She is carrying a pink and white checkered bag.

☐ **KEELY**
#1619
Issued 1998, Date purchased _____
Current, 7" tall
Market value: $19.95, paid $_____

Keely has long black hair with a blue ribbon. She is dressed in a green and white dress with white sleeves. She is carrying a blue and white checkered bag.

☐ **ZOE**
#1620
Issued 1998, Date purchased _____
Current, 7" tall
Market value: $19.95, paid $_____

Zoe has brown hair pulled up to the side of her head. She is wearing purple and white checkered dress with purple slacks. She is carrying a purple and white checkered bag.

☐ **BETSY**
#1657
Issued 1999, Date purchased _____
Current, 7" tall
Market value: $11.00, paid $_____

Betsy wears a light blue and white dress with white polka dots and matching light blue shoes. She is carrying a white purse.

☐ **PAULA**
#1658
Issued 1999, Date purchased _____
Current, 7" tall
Market value: $11.00, paid $_____

Paula is dressed in a pink and white dress with white polka dots. She has a blue ribbon around her waist and is wearing pink shoes. She is carrying a light blue purse.

GINA
#1659
Issued 1999, Date purchased _____
Current, 7" tall
Market value: $11.00, paid $_____

Gina has blond hair and is wearing an aqua and white dress
with a pink ribbon at the waistline and matching aqua shoes.
She is carrying a purse.

PAMELA
#1660
Issued 1999, Date purchased _____
Current, 7" tall
Market value: $11.00, paid $_____

Pamela has brown hair and is dressed in a lavender and
white dress with a blue ribbon at her waistline. She is
wearing matching shoes and carrying a purse.

JOSHUA
#1661
Issued 1999, Date purchased _____
Current, 7" tall
Market value: $11.00, paid $_____

Joshua is a handsome blond boy in brown slacks, a blue
shirt, and a black vest. He also has a yellow tie around his
neck and is wearing a pair of brown shoes.

FRIENDS FROM THE
FARM SERIES

☐ **JUDY WITH PAIL**
   #1373
Issued July 1998, Date purchased _____
Retired, 12" tall
Market value: $30.00 – 45.00, paid $ _____

Judy is wearing a blue and white denim dress, has long straight blond hair, blue eyes, and holds a bucket labeled "MILK."

☐ **MABEL WITH CORN**
   #1374
Issued July 1998, Date purchased _____
Retired, 12" tall
Market value: $30.00 – 45.00, paid $ _____

Mabel looks comfortable in her denim overalls. She is carrying an ear of corn, has curly brown hair pulled back in ponytails, and has freckles on her face.

☐ **LILLIAN WITH CHICK**
   #1375
Issued 1999, Date purchased _____
Current, 12" tall
Market value: $30.00 – 45.00, paid $ _____

Lillian is wearing a denim accented dress with a peach sweater, and has curly dark blond hair pullled back in a ponytail. She is carrying a baby chick in one hand and a bag of chicken feed in the other.

☐ **NORA WITH FLOWERS**
   #1376
Issued 1999, Date purchased _____
Current, 12" tall
Market value: $30.00 – 45.00, paid $ _____

Nora has long dark blond hair, brown eyes, and is wearing a pretty plaid dress and denim vest. She carries a bundle of roses.

GARDEN OF FRIENDS COLLECTION

First Edition

These sweet little dolls are the first editions in the Garden Of Friends Collection. Each doll comes with an accessory that matches the month she represents.

Back row, left to right: January, February, March, April
Front row, left to right: May, June, July, August, September, October, November, December

JASMINE – JANUARY
#1455
Issued 1994, Date purchased _____
Limited 15,000, 12" tall
Market value: $65.00 – 75.00,
paid $ _____

VIOLET – FEBRUARY
#1456
Issued 1994, Date purchased _____
Limited 15,000, 12" tall
Market value: $65.00 – 75.00,
paid $ _____

LILY – MARCH
#1457
Issued 1994, Date purchased _____
Limited 15,000, 12" tall
Market value: $65.00 – 75.00,
paid $ _____

DAISY – APRIL
#1458
Issued 1994, Date purchased _____
Limited 15,000, 12" tall
Market value: $65.00 – 75.00,
paid $ _____

☐ **IRIS – MAY**
#1459
Issued 1994, Date purchased _____
Limited 15,000, 12" tall
Market value: $65.00 – 75.00, paid $_____

☐ **ROSE – JUNE**
#1460
Issued 1994, Date purchased _____
Limited 15,000, 12" tall
Market value: $65.00 – 75.00, paid $ _____

☐ **PANSY – JULY**
#1461
Issued 1994, Date purchased _____
Limited 15,000, 12" tall
Market value: $65.00 – 75.00, paid $ _____

☐ **BLOSSOM – AUGUST**
#1462
Issued 1994, Date purchased _____
Limited 15,000, 12" tall
Market value: $65.00 – 75.00, paid $_____

☐ **SUNNY – SEPTEMBER**
#1463
Issued 1994, Date purchased _____
Limited 15,000, 12" tall
Market value: $65.00 – 75.00, paid $_____

☐ **PUMPKIN – OCTOBER**
#1464
Issued 1994, Date purchased _____
Limited 15,000, 12" tall
Market value: $65.00 – 75.00, paid $_____

☐ **CHRISSY – NOVEMBER**
#1465
Issued 1994, Date purchased _____
Limited 15,000, 12" tall
Market value: $65.00 – 75.00, paid $ _____

☐ **HOLLY – DECEMBER**
#1466
Issued 1994, Date purchased _____
Limited 15,000, 12" tall
Market value: $65.00 – 75.00, paid $ _____

Second Edition

Issued 1995; Limited 15,000; 12" tall; Market value: $39.95

These dolls are the second editions in the Garden of Friends Collection. They are dressed in the colors of the month for which they are named. Each doll holds a watering can with a picture of the flower that matches her name.

Top row, January through June. Bottom row, July through December.

☐ **JASMINE – JANUARY**
#1425
Date purchased_____
paid $ _____

☐ **VIOLET – FEBRUARY**
#1426
Date purchased_____
paid $ _____

☐ **LILY – MARCH**
#1427
Date purchased_____
paid $ _____

☐ **DAISY – APRIL**
#1428
Date purchased_____
paid $ _____

☐ **IRIS – MAY**
#1429
Date purchased_____
paid $ _____

☐ **ROSE – JUNE**
#1430
Date purchased_____
paid $ _____

☐ **PANSY – JULY**
#1431
Date purchased_____
paid $ _____

☐ **BLOSSOM – AUGUST**
#1432
Date purchased_____
paid $ _____

☐ **SUNNY – SEPTEMBER**
#1433
Date purchased_____
paid $ _____

☐ **PUMPKIN – OCTOBER**
#1434
Date purchased_____
paid $ _____

☐ **CHRISSY – NOVEMBER**
#1435
Date purchased_____
paid $ _____

☐ **HOLLY – DECEMBER**
#1436
Date purchased_____
paid $ _____

Third Edition

Issued 1997; Limited 15,000; 12" tall; Market value: $39.95

These dolls are the third editions in the Garden Of Friends Collection. The dolls' dresses feature the flowers from which their names are derived and each doll has an accessory.

Top row: January through June
Bottom row: July through December

☐ **JASMINE – JANUARY**
#1388
Date purchased _____
paid $ _____

☐ **BLUE BELL – FEBRUARY**
#1389
Date purchased _____
paid $ _____

☐ **MORNING GLORY – MARCH**
#1390
Date purchased _____
paid $ _____

☐ **LILY – APRIL**
#1391
Date purchased _____
paid $ _____

☐ **DAISY – MAY**
#1392
Date purchased _____
paid $ _____

☐ **ROSE – JUNE**
#1393
Date purchased _____
paid $ _____

☐ **PANSY – JULY**
#1394
Date purchased _____
paid $ _____

☐ **PEONY – AUGUST**
#1395
Date purchased _____
paid $ _____

☐ **SUNNY – SEPTEMBER**
#1396
Date purchased _____
paid $ _____

☐ **PUMPKIN – OCTOBER**
#1397
Date purchased _____
paid $ _____

☐ **MARIGOLD – NOVEMBER**
#1398
Date purchased _____
paid $ _____

☐ **HOLLY – DECEMBER**
#1399
Date purchased _____
paid $ _____

GENERAL LINE

☐ **JESSI**
#1001
Issued February 1989, Date purchased _____
Retired 1998, 16" tall
Market value: $125.00, paid $_____

Jessi is a gorgeous bride with a white satin gown and white veil.
She is holding a bouquet of flowers.

☐ **JONNY**
#1011
Issued 1996, Date purchased _____
Retired 1996, 16" – 17" tall
Market value: $75.00 – 85.00, paid $_____

This groom is ready to wed Jessi. He is dressed in his tuxedo, with satin shirt and
bow tie. He is also wearing a cummerbund under his jacket. Jonny was available
in three colors of suits: brown, gray, and black. This one comes with a black suit,
white shirt, and lavender tie.

☐ **JONNY**
#1011
Issued 1989, Date purchased _____
Retired 1998, 16" – 18" tall
Market value: $125.00 – 150.00, paid $_____

Brown suit, cream shirt, and yellow tie.

☐ **JONNY**
#1011
Issued 1989, Date purchased _____
Retired 1998, 16" – 17" tall
Market value: $100.00 – 125.00, paid $_____

Gray suit, white shirt, and lavender tie.

□ **MISSY – Pink**
#1003
Issued 1989, Date purchased _____
Retired 1995, 16" tall
Market value: $195.00 – 225.00, paid $ _____

Missy is wearing a pink satin dress and white pinafore. She has pink ribbons in her pigtails.

□ **OZARK ANNIE**
#1009
Issued September 1989, Date purchased _____
Retired 1992, 14½" – 15" tall
Market value: $225.00 – 250.00, paid $ _____

Ozark Annie is beautiful in her pink polka dot dress. She comes with a pink polka dot hat covering her pigtail braids. The first version of Annie came with pigtails, whereas the second version came with her hair in braids.

□ **OZARK ANDY**
#1010
Issued September 1989, Date purchased _____
Retired 1992, 14" – 14½" tall
Market value: $225 00 – 250.00, paid $ _____

Andy comes clad in a polka dot shirt and a pair of coveralls. He has on a large bow tie and his pants are cuffed. Andy has red hair.

□ **JENNY**
#1012
Issued 1990, Date purchased _____
Retired 1992, 14¾" – 15½" tall
Market value: $225.00 – 250.00, paid $ _____

This is a great doll for a bed. She wears a white lace christening gown and a bonnet with pink satin ribbons.

JORDAN
#1013
Issued 1990, Date purchased _____
Retired 1992, 14¾" – 16" tall
Market value: $200.00 – 225.00, paid $ _____

Jordan is wearing his white christening gown with white bonnet. The gown and bonnet have blue ribbons. A great doll for a bed.

TIFFANY
#1014
Issued March 1990, Date purchased _____
Retired 1995, 16" tall
Market value: $200.00 – 225.00, paid $ _____

Tiffany is a Southern Belle in a rose-colored dress and woven bonnet. Her two pigtails are adorned with roses and she is wearing a locket.

GIRL PAJAMA CLOWN
#1015
Issued 1991, Date purchased _____
Suspended 1994, 22" tall
Market value: $65.00 – 75.00, paid $ _____

This girl clown is dressed in a pink and white suit with a clown hat. She's made to be stuffed with a child's pajamas or tissue paper.

TIMMY THE ANGEL
#1017
Issued March 1990, Date purchased _____
Suspended 1992, 16" tall
Market value: $225.00 – 250.00, paid $ _____

Timmy is dressed in an angelic white robe with satin yellow ribbon. On his head is a golden halo and he has sandals on his feet.

TIMMY THE ANGEL
#1017A
Issued January 1992, Date purchased _____
Suspended 1994, 16" tall
Market value: $200.00 – 225.00, paid $ _____

Timmy is dressed in a heavenly blue gown holding his security blanket. He has a golden halo on his head.

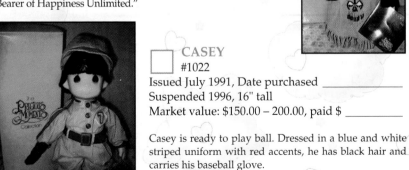

BOY PAJAMA CLOWN
#1018
Issued 1991, Date purchased _____
Suspended 1994, 22" tall
Market value: $65.00 – 75.00, paid $ _____

Boy Pajama Clown is dressed in a blue and yellow suit with a clown hat. He is made to be stuffed with a child's pajamas or tissue paper.

PRINCESS SINCERE
#1020
Issued October 1990, Date purchased _____
Limited edition 10,000; Retired 1993, 16" tall
Market value: $500.00 – 525.00, paid $ _____

Sincere is dressed in a Native American outfit, with blue beads in her headband and necklace. She has long black hair made into ponytails. Her beautiful thunderbird medallion means "Sacred Bearer of Happiness Unlimited."

CASEY
#1022
Issued July 1991, Date purchased _____
Suspended 1996, 16" tall
Market value: $150.00 – 200.00, paid $ _____

Casey is ready to play ball. Dressed in a blue and white striped uniform with red accents, he has black hair and carries his baseball glove.

COLIN
#1024
Issued November 1991, Date purchased _____
Suspended 1996, 16" tall
Market value: $100.00 – 125.00, paid $ _____

Colin is dressed in light blue pants, a pastel plaid shirt, and his favorite hat. He was named after one of Sam Butcher's grandsons.

KATIE
#1025
Issued November 1991, Date purchased _____
Retired 1996, 16" tall
Market value: $150.00 – 175.00, paid $ _____

Katie is ready for a Sunday outing in her pink jumper with a big plaid bow and pink polka dot blouse. She is wearing her wide brimmed hat covering her blond hair. She is named for one of Sam Butcher's granddaughters.

KERRI
#1026
Issued July 1991, Date purchased _____
Suspended 1993, 16" tall
Market value: $125.00 – 150.00, paid $_____

Kerri is clad in pastel stripes and a pink blouse. She has a pink bow on the topknot of her hair. She was named for one of Sam Butcher's granddaughters.

SANDY – Blue
#1031
Issued April 1992, Date purchased _____
Suspended 1994, 16" tall
Market value: $100.00 – 125.00, paid $ _____

This pretty blonde is ready for graduation in her royal blue gown and cap trimmed in gold. She has two blue bows in her hair.

SANDY – WHITE
#1032
Issued April 1992, Date purchased _____
Current, 16" tall
Market value: $50.00 – 55.00, paid $ _____

This pretty blonde is also ready for her graduation, wearing a white gown, white graduation cap, and white bows in her hair.

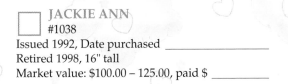

PHILIP
#1035
Issued October 1992, Date purchased _____
Retired 1994, 16" tall
Market value: $175.00 – 275.00, paid $ _____

Philip was created in memory of Philip Butcher, Sam's son, who died in an automobile accident in 1991. He comes with a dedication certificate. Philip is dressed in a patched shirt and blue jeans. He is wearing glasses (2,000 made with sunglasses) and denim sneakers. A slingshot is hanging out of his back pocket.

JACKIE ANN
#1038
Issued 1992, Date purchased _____
Retired 1998, 16" tall
Market value: $100.00 – 125.00, paid $ _____

Jackie Ann is wearing a blue cowgirl outfit with western boots. She looks stylish in her white western hat. She is riding her stick pony, Patch.

DUSTY
#1043
Issued 1993, Date purchased _____
Suspended 1996, 16" tall
Market value: $125.00 – 150.00, paid $ _____

Dusty is dressed in his train engineer overalls and hat. He is carrying his toy train, dreaming of becoming an engineer.

DELANEY
#1046
Issued 1997, Date purchased _____
Retired 1998, 16" tall
Market value: $75.00 – 100.00, paid $ _____

Delaney is dressed in a red and blue plaid dress with a matching plaid tam. She is carrying a basket of apples.

TRACEY
#1047
Issued 1993, Date purchased _____
Retired 1998, 16" tall
Market value: $95.00 – 125.00, paid $ _____

Tracey is ready for a baseball game sporting a pink and white striped uniform with a matching baseball cap. She has a baseball glove on her left hand.

MILLY AND HER NEW BABY DOLL
#1048
Issued 1993, Date purchased _____
Suspended 1993, 16" tall
Market value: $125.00 – 150.00, paid $ _____

Milly is dressed in a pink polka dot dress with blue polka dot sleeves and a white apron with lace. She is carrying a matching baby doll, which is in a box.

DAWN AND RAG DOLL
#1057
Issued 1993, Date purchased _____
Suspended 1996, 16" tall
Market value: $125.00 – 150.00, paid $ _____

Dawn is dressed in a pretty blue and cream nightgown with a matching nightcap. She is carrying her favorite rag doll.

VIOLA
#1062
Issued 1996, Date purchased _____
Suspended 2000, 16" tall
Market value: $50.00 – 65.00, paid $ _____

Viola comes in a violet and pink floral dress with a matching hair ribbon in her hair. She is also wearing matching leather shoes.

WHITE BABY
#1066
Issued 1993, Date purchased _____
Suspended 1996, 16" tall
Market value: $65.00 – 75.00, paid $ _____

This baby doll is dressed in a white sleeper gown with aqua polka dots and an aqua ribbon that ties at the bottom of the gown. The baby is wearing a little white cap, a one-piece suit under the gown, and white knit socks.

BROWN BABY
#1067A
Issued 1993, Date purchased _____
Suspended 1996, 16" tall
Market value: $65.00 – 75.00, paid $ _____

This baby doll is dressed the same as White Baby #1066, shown above.

AFRICAN-AMERICAN BABY
#1067B
Issued April 1997, Date purchased _____
Limited 500, Retired, 16" tall
Market value: $95.00 – 105.00, paid $ _____

This baby is in the same white gown as the other baby above but it had a limited production. The tag with this baby says "Brown Baby."

☐ **EVIE**
#1068
Issued 1994, Date purchased _____
Suspended 1995, 16" tall
Market value: $65.00 – 75.00, paid $ _____

Evie is elegant in her white blouse, black skirt, and red cummerbund. She has a black bow and red roses in her hair. She is holding a large golden snowflake.

☐ **SARAH**
#1074
Issued 1996, Date purchased _____
Retired 1998, 16" tall
Market value: $85.00 – 105.00, paid $ _____

This Amish girl is dressed in a simple black dress with a white cover. She also is wearing a white bonnet.

☐ **GRANDMA MARTHA**
#1085
Issued 1996, Date purchased _____
Suspended 1998, 16" tall
Market value: $100.00 – 125.00, paid $ _____

Grandma Martha is wearing a flower and vegetable dress and pretty green and white coat. She comes with a gardening hat, pair of glasses, and a watering can.

☐ **ELLIE**
#1086
Issued 1995, Date purchased _____
Suspended 1997, 16" tall
Market value: $55.00 – 65.00, paid $ _____

Ellie is dressed in a pink floral print and eyelet dress. She has a pink hat on her head.

COLLEEN
#1089
Issued 1995, Date purchased _____
Suspended 1997, 16" tall
Market value: $55.00 – 65.00, paid $ _____

Red-headed Colleen is wearing a dark green floral jumper with a white blouse, lace stockings, and leather-like shoes. She is carrying some shamrocks for St. Patrick's Day.

MISSY – 2nd EDITION
#1092
Issued 1995, Date purchased _____
Suspended 1998, 16" tall
Market value: $55.00 – 65.00, paid $ _____

Second edition Missy has a different style pink dress than #1003 on page 91. Her hair is also different, with a big pink bow on the top. In addition, she has a big pink bow around her waistline.

MISSY – 3rd EDITION
#1093
Issued 1998, Date purchased _____
Suspended 2000, 16" tall
Market value: $55.00 – 65.00, paid $ _____

This Missy is in a dark blue dress with eyelet white lace accents. Her hair is pulled up into a bun on the left side of her head.

MARGARET
#1094
Issued 1996, Date purchased _____
Retired 1998, 16" tall
Market value: $75.00 – 100.00, paid $ _____

Margaret's school uniform is a green, blue, red, and white plaid dress, white blouse, and navy blue vest. She is holding an ABC book in her hand. She has her hair tied up with a pretty blue ribbon and wears ankle socks and navy shoes.

JESUS LOVES ME (GIRL)
#1097
Issued 1998, Date purchased _____
Suspended 2000, 16" tall
Market value: $50.00 – 65.00, paid $ _____

This little blonde is wearing a pretty pink blouse with a dark pink skirt. Her shoes are blue and she has a dark pink ribbon in her hair. She is carrying a stuffed bunny.

JESUS LOVES ME (BOY)
#1098
Issued 1998, Date purchased _____
Suspended 2000, 16" tall
Market value: $50.00 – 65.00, paid $ _____

This little blond boy dressed in a blue shirt and navy blue pants is wearing white shoes and is carrying a stuffed teddy bear.

CHRISTENING
#1099
Issued 1998, Date purchased _____
Current, 16" tall
Market value: $75.00, paid $_____

This baby is wearing a gorgeous white satin gown trimmed in white lace. She is wearing a matching christening hat. She comes with a pillow that can be personalized by Precious Moments if you send in the postcard.

GRACIE
#1100
Issued 1996, Date purchased _____
Limited 1 year production, 16" tall
Market value: $50.00, paid $_____

Gracie wears a blue calico print dress with blue shoes to match. She also has matching ribbons in her pigtails.

GRAMMA'S SWEETIE
#1104
Issued 1996, Date purchased _____
Suspended 1998, 16" tall
Market value: $55.00 – 100.00, paid $ _____

The first 1,000 of these dolls had hats and dresses made of navy blue tricot; the rest were made in cotton. She is carrying a ticket to Gramma's house.

PIPER
#1107
Issued 1997, Date purchased _____
Current, 16" tall
Market value: $40.00, paid $_____

Piper the ballerina is dressed in a pink net dress with pink bows and white shoes with pink bows.

CAUCASIAN BABY
#1108
Issued 1997, Date purchased _____
Retired 1999, 16" tall
Market value: $45.00 – 55.00, paid $_____

HISPANIC BABY
#1109
Issued 1997, Date purchased _____
Retired 1999, 16" tall
Market value: $45.00 – 55.00, paid $_____

AFRICAN-AMERICAN BABY
#1117
Issued 1997, Date purchased _____
Retired 1999, 16" tall
Market value: $45.00 – 55.00, paid $ _____

All three of these baby dolls are dressed in white sleepers with pink rosebud print. They each have a cap to match the sleeper. Under their gowns the babies are wearing one-piece jumpsuits with white yokes accented by appliqué rose clusters. The babies all have little white diapers underneath their sleepers. Hispanic Baby was introduced first, followed by African-American Baby and finally, Caucasian Baby.

☐ **PAT**
#1114
Issued 1997, Date purchased _____
Suspended 2000, 16" tall
Market value: $45.00, paid $_____

Pat comes in a pretty floral dress with eyelet trim. She has shoulder length brown hair. She is carrying a pink embroidery hoop.

☐ **CUDDLES**
#1116
Issued 1998, Date purchased _____
Current, 16" tall
Market value: $40.00, paid $_____

Cuddles is dressed in a soft white lamb outfit. She has short curly blond hair and big blue teardrop eyes.

☐ **GRANDPA BILL**
#1118
Issued 1997, Date purchased _____
Suspended 1998, 16" tall
Market value: $60.00 – 75.00, paid $ _____

Bill is a cute boy doll with light blond hair. He is wearing a hat, glasses, gray pants, and a sweater. He holds a Precious Moments newspaper in his hand.

☐ **VAYA CON DIOS**
#1126
Issued 1998, Date purchased _____
Suspended 2000, 16" tall
Market value: $49.95, paid $_____

Vaya Con Dios is a beautiful Latin doll with long black curly hair, dark skin, and brown eyes. She is wearing a gorgeous pink lace gown, pink satin pantaloons, and pink satin shoes.

CHARITY
#1127
Issued 1998, Date purchased _____
Closed 2000, 16" tall
Market value: $49.95, paid $_____

Charity is wearing a long cream colored floral dress with matching hat and has dark blond curly hair. The doll's proceeds were donated to the Ronald McDonald House of the Four States in 1999.

TARA
#1128
Issued 1998, Date purchased _____
Suspended 2000, 16" tall
Market value: $50.00 – 75.00, paid $ _____

Tara has blond hair and almost teal colored eyes. This doll wears a dark green velvet skirt and matching hat, a Christmas print blouse and jacket, and vinyl ice skates.

BRITTANY
#1131
Issued 1998, Date purchased _____
Suspended 2000, 16" tall
Market value: $45.00 – 50.00, paid $ _____

Brittany is a lovely African-American doll with a precious long green, pink, and white calico print dress. She has long curly black hair that is parted on the side and is adorned with a matching bow.

ANGEL
#1135
Issued 1999, Date purchased _____
Limited 1,000, 16" tall
Market value: $75.00 – 100.00, paid $ _____

Angel has brown hair and wears a long lavender gown with a big lavender bow and a little pink heart at the neckline. She has a matching lavender bonnet.

PAW
#1140
Issued 1999, Date purchased _____
Current, 16" tall
Market value: $39.95, paid $_____

Paw's brown teddy bear costume is complete with a tail, ears, and paws. He has a white and blue polka dot bow at his neck.

ANNIE
#1143
Issued January 2000, Date purchased _____
Suspended 2000, 16" tall
Market value: $39.95, paid $_____

Annie has black hair styled in two braids, brown eyes, and wears a blue denim jumpsuit over a pink and white checkered blouse. She also wears white and pink tennis shoes.

BARBARA JOHNSON
#1145
Issued January 2000, Date purchased _____
1 year production, 16" tall
Market value: $59.95, paid $_____

Barbara Johnson is dressed in a long purple dress. She has brunette hair and brown eyes. She is wearing a straw hat decorated with red geraniums and holds a spatula in her hand.

JEREMY
#1147
Issued April 2000, Date purchased _____
Suspended 2001, 16" tall
Market value: $44.95, paid $_____

Jeremy has dark brown hair, blue eyes, and is an angel ready to shoot some hoops. He was created in honor of a real teenager named Jeremy that died in a car accident.

JENNA
#1148

Issued September 2000, Date purchased _____
Current, 16" tall
Market value: $39.95, paid $ _____

Jenna is wearing a dark blue skirt, a jacket with hood and matching muff, and white ice skates. She has dark blond hair and brown eyes.

YOSHIKO
#1212

Issued April 2001, Date purchased _____
Current, 16" tall
Market value: $49.95, paid $_____

Yoshiko is an Oriental doll wearing a stunning authentic red silk Japanese kimono. She has pretty black hair.

THE CHRISTENING
#1291

Issued October 2002, Date purchased _____
Current, 16" tall
Market value: $80.00, paid $ _____

The Christening doll is dressed in a pure white satin christening gown with lace overlay, which makes her 30" long. She has pretty blond hair with a matching white satin bonnet.

TOOTH FAIRY
#1301

Issued April 1999, Date purchased _____
Current, 12" tall
Market value: $29.95, paid $_____

Tooth Fairy comes with wings that velcro onto her back. She also has a wand and a bag in which to carry teeth. She wears a pretty blue and white dress.

BUTTONS
#1305
Issued 1999, Date purchased _____
Limited 5,000, 12" tall
Market value: $34.95, paid $_____

Buttons is dressed in blue and tan coveralls with a tan and blue polka dot top. He has a tan hat on his head. His hair is a light blue color.

COTTON CANDY
#1306
Issued 1999, Date purchased _____
Limited 5,000, 12" tall
Market value: $34.95, paid $_____

Cotton Candy is dressed in a lavender and tan jumper. She has a lavender hat on her head. Her hair is also lavender.

BILLY
#1307
Issued April 1999, Date purchased _____
Current, 12" tall
Market value: $29.95, paid $_____

Billy is ready for bed in his light blue pajamas with a matching cap and light blue slippers on his feet. He is kneeling to say his nightly prayers.

SALLY
#1308
Issued April 1999, Date purchased _____
Current, 12" tall
Market value: $29.95, paid $_____

Sally is dressed in a cream flowered nightgown, with a matching cream cap. She has pink slippers on her feet and is kneeling for her nightly prayers.

Millennium Angels include certificates of authenticity, special doll boxes, and are mounted on their own wood stands. Choose the Angel of the North (blond hair and blue eyes, front row), Angel of the West (dark blond hair and blue eyes, middle row, left), Angel of the South (black hair and brown eyes, middle row, right), or Angel of the East (black hair and brown eyes, back row).

☐ **NORTH MILLENNIUM ANGEL**
#1317
Issued April 1999, Date purchased _____
1 year production, 12" tall
Market value: $39.95, paid $_____

☐ **SOUTH MILLENNIUM ANGEL**
#1318
Issued April 1999,
Date purchased _____
1 year production, 12" tall
Market value: $39.95, paid $_____

☐ **EAST MILLENNIUM ANGEL**
#1319
Issued April 1999,
Date purchased _____
1 year production, 12" tall
Market value: $39.95, paid $_____

☐ **WEST MILLENNIUM ANGEL**
#1320
Issued April 1999,
Date purchased _____
1 year production, 12" tall
Market value: $39.95, paid $_____

☐ **PEGGY JEAN**
#1326
Issued January 2000, Date purchased _____
Current, 12" tall
Market value: $29.95, paid $_____

Peggy Jean is dressed for square dancing in her flowered dress with pink lace. She has blond hair with two curls on the side of her head.

☐ **JESS**
#1327
Issued January 2000, Date purchased _____
Current, 12" tall
Market value: $29.95, paid $_____

Jess is also dressed for square dancing in his blue denim pants and handsome blue shirt and a big black cowboy hat on his head.

☐ **NANCY**
#1328
Issued January 2000, Date purchased _____
Current, 12" tall
Market value: $29.95, paid $_____

Nancy has green eyes and wears her lucky fishing outfit: blue denim coveralls with a green blouse and a matching blue hat. She comes with a fishing pole and a fish.

These are the Precious Moments Graduation dolls that can be personalized. Choose blond or brunette, the color tassel that you want (red, blue, green, black, purple, or orange), and up to ten characters that can be embroidered right on the collar. Each doll is wearing a white satin robe and matching cap.

☐ **BLOND GRADUATE**
#1331
Issued January 2000,
Date purchased _____
Current, 12" tall
Market value: $31.00, paid $ _____

☐ **BRUNETTE GRADUATE**
#1332
Issued January 2000,
Date purchased _____
Current, 12" tall
Market value: $31.00, paid $_____

☐ **MADISON**
#1339
Issued January 2000, Date purchased _____
Current, 12" tall
Market value: $59.95, paid $_____

Madison has dark blond hair, brown eyes, and is wearing the most adorable outfit made of black crushed faux velvet with animal fur print trim. She even has a matching purse.

LAUREN
#1340
Issued January 2000, Date purchased _____
Current, 12" tall
Market value: $29.95, paid $_____

Lauren has brown hair, brown eyes, and wears a Scottish plaid outfit with matching purse that is decorated with black Scottish terries.

KYLIE
#1341
Issued September 2000, Date purchased _____
Current, 12" tall
Market value: $29.95, paid $_____

Kylie has blond curls, blue eyes, wears lavender pajamas, and is carrying a yellow blanket. She has jointed/moveable arms and legs.

KARISSA
#1348
Issued September 2000, Date purchased _____
Current, 12" tall
Market value: $29.95, paid $_____

Karissa has blond hair, blue eyes, and wears a beautiful light green and lavender dress. She is holding a carousel horse.

☐ **KYLIE**
#1341A
Issued October 2002,
Date purchased _____
Current, 12" tall
Market value: $32.00, paid $ _____

Kylie has long curly hair with lavender ribbons. She is wearing a purple sleeper and is carrying a yellow blanket.

☐ **KEKE**
#4129
Issued October 2002,
Date purchased _____
Current, 9" tall
Market value: $24.00, paid $_____

Keke has blond hair with a lavender bow. She is wearing a cozy yellow sleeper and carrying a purple blanket.

☐ **UPTOWN GIRL**
#1365
Issued 2002, Date purchased _____
Current, 12" tall
Market value: $31.00, paid $_____

Uptown Girl features a red and black plaid skirt with a red sweater. She has black shoes and white stockings. She has brown hair pulled up with red ribbons. She is carrying a red purse that can be personalized.

☐ **ALL VINYL BABY DOLL**
#1368
Issued 2002, Date purchased _____
Current, 12" tall
Market value: $25.00, paid $_____

This cute little baby came with three different outfits (diaper, romper, and pajamas). The pajamas and romper are in matching prints. He is also wearing a matching print cap.

These little African-American dolls are dressed in cheerleader uniforms with pompoms and megaphones. They come in many colors: blue, orange, red, green, yellow, and purple. These dolls can be personalized. Cheerleaders also came in Brunette (#1372) and Blond (#1472) versions.

☐ **CHEERLEADER –
AFRICAN-AMERICAN**
#1370B
Issued 1997, Date purchased _____
Current, 12" tall
Market value: $31.00, paid $_____

☐ **CHEERLEADER –
AFRICAN-AMERICAN**
#1370P
Issued 1997, Date purchased _____
Current, 12" tall
Market value: $31.00, paid $_____

These little brunette dolls are dressed in cheerleader uniforms with pompoms and megaphones. They come in many colors: blue, orange, red, green, yellow, and purple. These dolls can be personalized. Cheerleaders also came in African-American (#1370) and Blond (#1472) versions.

☐ **BRUNETTE CHEERLEADER – RED**
#1372R
Issued 1998, Date purchased _____
Current, 12" tall
Market value: $31.00, paid $_____

☐ **BRUNETTE CHEERLEADER – BLUE**
#1372B
Issued 1998, Date purchased _____
Current, 12" tall
Market value: $31.00, paid $_____

☐ **BRUNETTE CHEERLEADER –
ORANGE**
#1372O
Issued 1998, Date purchased _____
Current, 12" tall
Market value: $31.00, paid $_____

☐ **BRUNETTE CHEERLEADER –
GREEN**
#1372G
Issued 1998, Date purchased _____
Current, 12" tall
Market value: $31.00, paid $_____

☐ **BRUNETTE CHEERLEADER –
PURPLE**
#1372P
Issued 1999, Date purchased _____
Current, 12" tall
Market value: $31.00, paid $_____

☐ **BRUNETTE CHEERLEADER –
YELLOW**
#1372Y
Issued 1998, Date purchased _____
Current, 12" tall
Market value: $31.00, paid $_____

LOLLIPOP
#1378
Issued 1998, Date purchased _____
Limited 7,500, 12" tall
Market value: $99.95, paid $ _____

Lolllipop has blond curly hair and is carrying a lollipop in her hand. She has painted blush on her cheeks, a bright and ornate satin outfit, and a festive hat.

POM POM
#1377
Issued 1998, Date purchased _____
Limited 7,500, 12" tall
Market value: $34.95, paid $ _____

Pom Pom has been produced with painted blush on his cheeks, a bright and ornate satin outfit, curly hair, and a festive hat. Pom Pom has purple hair and is decked with pompoms on his outfit.

GUARDIAN ANGEL
#1412
Issued 1996, Date purchased _____
Suspended January 2001, 12" tall
Market value: $35.00 – 50.00, paid $ _____

Guardian Angel is a blue-eyed blond boy with a white satin angelic gown that is adorned with patches. He has a golden halo made of cord and white sandals to complete the angel outfit.

Groom is dressed in a basic black suit with lavender bow tie and Bride is wearing a beautiful white gown with a white veil and holds a bouquet of flowers.

BLOND BRIDE
#1421
Issued 1997, Date purchased _____
Current, 12" tall
Market value: $29.95, paid $_____

BLOND GROOM
#1422
Issued 1997, Date purchased _____
Current, 12" tall
Market value: $29.95, paid $_____

ANGELA
#1439
Issued 1996, Date purchased _____
Suspended January 2001, 12" tall
Market value: $29.95, paid $_____

Angela's a praying, little brown-eyed, dark blond with a pink/mauve floral print dress. In 1998 her dress was slightly changed to a different floral print.

HALEY
#1449
Issued 1997, Date purchased _____
Current, 12" tall
Market value: $29.95, paid $_____

Haley is a sweet redhead, has long braids, and is wearing a pretty green satin dress with lace trim. She has a special green name tag attached to her arm with a picture of a shamrock on it.

CINDY — 2nd EDITION
#1450
Issued 1998, Date purchased _____
Current, 12" tall
Market value: $29.95, paid $_____

Cindy comes in a blue and white checkered dress and is jumping rope. Cindy 2nd Edition dolls are made available to Precious Moments retailers not by the regular wholesale market, but strictly through the Precious Moments Company's tele-marketing department.

CLIFFORD
#1467
Issued 1994, Date purchased _____
Suspended 1998, 12" tall
Market value: $34.95, paid $_____

Clifford carries a toy bunny and is wearing a light blue shorts-jumpsuit with fish accents. He is also wearing a matching blue coat and hat.

WINNIE
#1468
Issued 1994, Date purchased _____
Suspended 1998, 12" tall
Market value: $34.95, paid $_____

Winnie is a red-headed little girl with a floral dress, white hat, and a pink coat. She carries a basket of eggs.

HAPPY THE CLOWN
#1470
Issued 2001, Date purchased _____
Current, 12" tall
Market value: $30.00, paid $_____

Happy is a cute little clown wearing a lavender, gold, and blue clown outfit with two green puff ball buttons. He is also wearing a matching hat and shoes.

These little blond dolls are dressed in cheerleader uniforms with pompoms and megaphones. They come in many colors: blue, orange, red, green, yellow, and purple. These dolls can be personalized. Cheerleaders also came in Brunette (#1372) and African-American (#1370) versions.

☐ **BLOND CHEERLEADER – BLUE**
#1472B
Issued 1998, Date purchased _____
Current, 12" tall
Market value: $31.00, paid $_____

☐ **BLOND CHEERLEADER – RED**
#1472R
Issued 1998, Date purchased _____
Current, 12" tall
Market value: $31.00, paid $_____

☐ **BLOND CHEERLEADER – GREEN**
#1472G
Issued 1998, Date purchased _____
Current, 12" tall
Market value: $31.00, paid $_____

☐ **BLOND CHEERLEADER – ORANGE**
#1472O
Issued 1998, Date purchased _____
Current, 12" tall
Market value: $31.00, paid $_____

BLOND CHEERLEADER – PURPLE
#1472P
Issued 1999, Date purchased _____
Current, 12" tall
Market value: $31.00, paid $_____

BLOND CHEERLEADER – YELLOW
#1472Y
Issued 1998, Date purchased _____
Current, 12" tall
Market value: $31.00, paid $_____

CHRISTINA
#1490
Issued 1996, Date purchased _____
Current, 12" tall
Market value: $31.00, paid $ _____

Christina is dressed for her First Communion. She has on an elegant white dress with matching shoes and socks. On her long blond hair rests a white veil.

GRACE
#1491
Issued 1995, Date purchased _____
Current, 12" tall
Market value: $31.00, paid $ _____

Grace is dressed for her First Communion. She has on a lovely white dress with matching shoes and socks. On her long brunette hair is a white veil.

CHRISTINA
#1490N
Issued October 2002, Date purchased _____
Current, 12" tall
Market value: $32.00, paid $_____

Christina has beautiful short blond hair with a white veil on her head. She is dressed for her First Communion in white satin and lace. Her satin purse can be monogrammed.

GRACE
#1491N
Issued October 2002, Date purchased _____
Current, 12" tall
Market value: $32.00, paid $_____

Grace has beautiful brunette hair with a white veil on her head. She is dressed for her First Communion in a dress of white satin and lace. Her satin purse can be monogrammed.

Groom is dressed in a basic black suit with lavender bow tie and Bride is wearing a beautiful white gown with a white veil and holds a bouquet of flowers.

BRUNETTE BRIDE
#1492
Issued 1995, Date purchased _____
Current, 12" tall
Market value: $29.95, paid $_____

BRUNETTE GROOM
#1493
Issued 1995, Date purchased _____
Current, 12" tall
Market value: $29.95, paid $_____

YOUNG HEE
#1498
Issued 1997, Date purchased _____
Suspended 1999, 12" tall
Market value: $29.95, paid $_____

Young Hee is a black haired girl dressed for her karate lesson in her white uniform. She has a black belt around her waist.

YOUNG HO
#1499
Issued 1997, Date purchased _____
Suspended 1999, 12" tall
Market value: $29.95, paid $_____

Young Ho is a black haired boy dressed for his karate lesson in his white uniform. He has a black belt around his waist.

WHITE GRADUATION
#1554
Issued 1997, Date purchased _____
Suspended 2000, 9" tall
Market value: $21.00, paid $_____

This little doll is dressed in her white graduation gown with a matching cap that has a yellow tassel. She has short blond hair and blue eyes.

DONNA
#1556
Issued 1998, Date purchased _____
Suspended January 2001, 9" tall
Market value: $21.00, paid $_____

Donna is ready for a wedding as the flower girl in a pretty pink and cream dress. She is carrying a basket of flowers. She has brown hair accented with roses.

☐ **DANNY**
#1557
Issued 1998, Date purchased _____
Suspended January 2001, 9" tall
Market value: $21.00, paid $_____

Danny is dressed for a wedding as the ringbearer in a handsome cream tuxedo with a pink bow tie. He is carrying a pillow with a wedding ring on it.

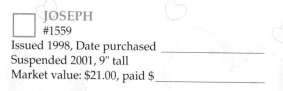

☐ **JOSEPH**
#1559
Issued 1998, Date purchased _____
Suspended 2001, 9" tall
Market value: $21.00, paid $_____

Joseph is dressed in a technicolor coat and white and red ancient gown. On his head is a red cap. He is one of the main characters of the Precious Moments cartoons.

☐ **SCARECROW BOY**
#1560
Issued 1998, Date purchased _____
Suspended January 2001, 9" tall
Market value: $21.00, paid $_____

This little boy is dressed in a pair of blue denim jeans, white tee-shirt, plaid shirt, and a straw hat. He has straw sticking out of his waistline and pants cuffs.

MR. & MRS. NOAH WITH TWO LAMBS
#1565
Issued 1998, Date purchased _____
Current, 9" tall
Market value: $44.95, paid $_____

Mr. & Mrs. Noah come with two lambs. Both are dressed in ancient garments. Mr. Noah is dressed in a light blue and cream outfit and Mrs. Noah is dressed in a printed gown with a pink garment on her head.

SCARECROW GIRL
#1570
Issued April 2000, Date purchased _____
Current, 9" tall
Market value: $21.00, paid $_____

This pretty little girl is wearing a blue denim dress with white lace. On her head is a straw hat. She is carrying a bag of birdseed and a bird sits on her left hand.

SANDY
#1571
Issued January 2000, Date purchased _____
Current, 9" tall
Market value: $21.00, paid $_____

Sandy has dark blond hair and brown eyes. She is dressed in a red and light blue bathing suit with a matching hat and is carrying a bucket and shovel. Also around her waist is a yellow and green inner tube with hearts.

PUMPKIN (MICHAEL)
#1573
Issued April 2000, Date purchased _____
Current, 9" tall
Market value: $21.00, paid $_____

Pumpkin is dressed in his Halloween pumpkin outfit of orange and green, with a green hat. He is carrying a trick or treat bag.

PILGRIM BOY
#1574
Issued 2000, Date purchased _____
Current, 9" tall
Market value: $21.00, paid $ _____

Pilgrim Boy is wearing a black, gray, and white pilgrim outfit with a matching black hat. He has black shoes with big buckles on them. He comes with a pumpkin.

PILGRIM GIRL
#1575
Issued 2000, Date purchased _____
Current, 9" tall
Market value: $21.00, paid $ _____

Pilgrim Girl is dressed in a black, gray, and white outfit, with a floral design on the top. She has a white apron and a white and gray bonnet. She comes with a basket.

TORI
#1578
Issued September 2000,
Date purchased _____
Current, 9" tall
Market value: $21.00, paid $ _____

Tori is a ballerina with blond hair wearing a white tutu and a pair of white leotards. She has her hair up in white beads.

MARIELLE
#1577
Issued September 2000,
Date purchased _____
Current, 9" tall
Market value: $21.00, paid $ _____

Marielle is a ballerina with brunette hair wearing a purple tutu and a pair of white leotards. She has her hair up in purple beads.

OZARK ANNIE
#1601
Issued 1990, Date purchased _____
Retired 1992, 26" tall
Market value: $600.00 – 650.00, paid $ _____

This beautiful girl wears a pink polka dot dress and she comes with a pink polka dot hat covering her pigtails or braids. The first version of Annie came with pigtails, whereas the second version came with her hair in braids.

OZARK ANDY
#1602
Issued 1990, Date purchased _____
Retired 1992, 26" tall
Market value: $600.00 – 650.00, paid $ _____

Andy comes wearing a polka dot shirt, a pair of coveralls, and a large bow tie. His pants come cuffed. Andy's hair is red.

JESSI
#1603
Issued 1989, Date purchased _____
Suspended 1992, 26" tall
Market value: $400.00 – 450.00, paid $ _____

This gorgeous bride is radiant in her white satin gown and veil. She is holding a bouquet of flowers.

JONNY
#1604
Issued 1989, Date purchased _____
Suspended 1992, 26" tall
Market value: $375.00 – 400.00, paid $ _____

Jonny groom is ready to wed Jessi. He is in his tuxedo with a cream satin shirt and blue bow tie. He is also wearing a cummerbund under his jacket.

BLOND BRIDE
#1621
Issued 1998, Date purchased _____
Current, 7" tall
Market value: $12.95, paid $_____

This bride is gorgeous in her white bridal gown and white veil. She is carrying a bouquet of flowers. She and Blond Groom below are perfect for a wedding cake top.

BLOND GROOM
#1622
Issued 1998, Date purchased _____
Current, 7" tall
Market value: $12.95, paid $_____

The handsome little groom is dressed in a black tuxedo with white shirt and black bow tie. He and Blond Bride #1621 are perfect for a wedding cake top.

LIL' PUMKIN
#1640
Issued October 2002, Date purchased _____
Current, 7" tall
Market value: $15.00, paid $_____

Lil' Pumkin is dressed for a night of trick-or-treating in her pumpkin costume. She has long bright orange hair with a green leaf hat.

AFRICAN–AMERICAN BRIDE
#1653
Issued 1999, Date purchased _____
Current, 7" tall
Market value: $12.95, paid $_____

African-American Bride is wearing a beautiful white bridal gown with a white veil. She is carrying a bouquet of flowers. She and African-American Groom on the next page are perfect for a wedding cake top.

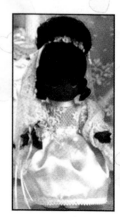

AFRICAN–AMERICAN GROOM
#1654
Issued 1999, Date purchased _____
Current, 7" tall
Market value: $12.95, paid $_____

African-American Groom is dressed in a black tuxedo with a white shirt and black bow tie. He and African-American Bride are perfect for the top of a wedding cake.

BRUNETTE BRIDE
#1655
Issued 1999, Date purchased _____
Current, 7" tall
Market value: $12.95, paid $_____

Brunette Bride wears a beautiful white bridal gown and veil. She is carrying a bouquet of flowers, and is perfect for a wedding cake top, along with Brunette Groom.

BRUNETTE GROOM
#1656
Issued 1999, Date purchased _____
Current, 7" tall
Market value: $12.95, paid $_____

Handsome little Brunette Groom is dressed in a black tuxedo with a white shirt and black bow tie. He and Brunette Bride would look great together on top of a wedding cake.

HEATHER
#1708
Issued 1990, Date purchased _____
Current, 16" tall
Market value: $39.95, paid $_____

Heather has big blue eyes, short blond curly hair, and is wearing a plush pink bunny suit. The outfit is attached with velcro and the fuzzy shoes also come apart, with velcro attachments.

JOSH
#1709
Issued 1990, Date purchased _____
Retired 1991, 16" tall
Market value: $175.00 – 200.00, paid $ _____

Josh has big blue eyes, short blond straight hair, and is wearing a plush blue bunny suit. The outfit is attached with velcro and the fuzzy shoes also come apart, with velcro attachments.

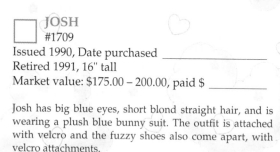

JEREMY
#1722
Issued 1994, Date purchased _____
Retired 1999, 16" tall
Market value: $100.00 – 125.00, paid $ _____

Jeremy has big blue eyes, short blond straight hair, and is wearing a plush white bunny suit. The outfit is attached with velcro and the fuzzy shoes also come apart, with velcro attachments.

☐ **BLUE TEDDY BEAR**
#1741
Issued 1991, Date purchased _____
Discontinued December 1992, 12" tall
Market value: $100.00 – 125.00,
paid $ _____

This adorable blue bear wears its heart on
its right hand. The heart reads, "Squeeze
Me," and if you squeeze it, you will hear it
squeak. It's the little bear's way of saying,
"I Love You, Too!"

☐ **PINK TEDDY BEAR**
#1740
Issued 1991, Date purchased _____
Discontinued December 1992, 12" tall
Market value: $100.00 – 125.00,
paid $_____

This pink bear wears its heart on its right
hand. The heart reads, "Squeeze Me," and
if you squeeze it, you will hear it squeak.
It's the little bear's way of saying, "I Love
You, Too!"

These cute little dolls are wearing
Halloween costumes: bunny, duck,
and bee. Each doll has straight blond
hair.

☐ **BEATRICE – BEE**
#1752
Issued 2001, Date purchased _____
Current, 12" tall
Market value: $34.95, paid $ _____

☐ **BELINDA – BUNNY**
#1753
Issued 2001, Date purchased _____
Current, 12" tall
Market value: $34.95, paid $ _____

☐ **DAPHNE – DUCK**
#1754
Issued 2001, Date purchased _____
Current, 12" tall
Market value: $34.95, paid $_____

LEAH THE LADYBUG
#1755
Issued August 2002, Date purchased _____
Current, 12" tall
Market value: $20.00, paid $_____

Leah is dressed for Halloween in her ladybug costume. She
has blond hair.

HUNTER THE HOUND DOG
#1756
Issued August 2002, Date purchased _____
Current, 12" tall
Market value: $20.00, paid $_____

Hunter is dressed for Halloween in his hound dog costume.
He has black hair.

FELICITY THE FELINE
#1759
Issued August 2002, Date purchased _____
Current, 12" tall
Market value: $20.00, paid $_____

Felicity is dressed for Halloween in her cat costume. She
has blond hair.

MADDIE
#4111
Issued October 2002, Date purchased _____
Current, 12" tall
Market value: $34.00, paid $_____

Maddie is dressed in a black and leopard print coat with a
matching hat. She is carrying a little doll dressed in matching
clothes. She has long curly blond hair.

HEARTS
#4213
Issued 2002, Date purchased _____
Current, 12" tall
Market value: $35.00, paid $_____

Hearts wears a yellow clown outfit with pink hearts. She has big pink shoes on her feet and a white hat on her head. She has purple yarn hair and is carrying a heart.

STRIPES
#4214
Issued 2002, Date purchased _____
Current, 12" tall
Market value: $35.00, paid $_____

Stripes is dressed in a white and purple striped clown outfit accented with yellow pompoms. He is wearing a matching striped hat with a green pompom on the top. He has light blue yarn hair and is wearing yellow and light blue shoes.

ROSE – ROSES ARE RED
#4231
Issued August 2002,
Date purchased _____
Current, 12" tall
Market value: $32.00, paid $_____

Rose is dressed in a beautiful red velvet dress accented with red roses. She is wearing a matching hat with red rose accents. She has short straight blond hair.

VIOLET – VIOLETS ARE BLUE
#4232
Issued August 2002,
Date purchased _____
Current, 12" tall
Market value: $32.00, paid $_____

Violet is dressed in a dark purple dress with violet flower accents. She is wearing a matching hat accented with purple violets. She has short straight blond hair.

LAZY SUSAN
#4242
Issued August 2002, Date purchased _____
Current, 12" tall
Market value: $32.00, paid $_____

Susan is dressed in a blue and white checkered jumper with a matching hat with a large sunflower. She has long blond ponytails with yellow ribbons.

SINGING IN THE RAIN
#4243
Issued October 2002, Date purchased _____
Current, 12" tall
Market value: $38.00, paid $_____

This cutie is dressed in a yellow rain coat with sunflower accents, yellow boots, and matching rain hat. Her dress under the coat is also accented with sunflowers. She is carrying a yellow umbrella and has curly brown hair.

SUNFLOWER SALLY
#4244
Issued October 2002, Date purchased _____
Current, 12" tall
Market value: $32.00, paid $_____

Sally's outfit consists of a blue and white checkered dress with white lace trim and sunflower accents around the arms, and a straw hat with a sunflower. She has long brown ponytails.

NATASHA – AT THE ICE RINK
#4251
Issued October 2002, Date purchased _____
Current, 12" tall
Market value: $32.00, paid $_____

Natasha wears a light blue dress with white fur trim, white fur band, and light blue bow around her head. She is wearing a pair of white ice skates and has long curly black hair.

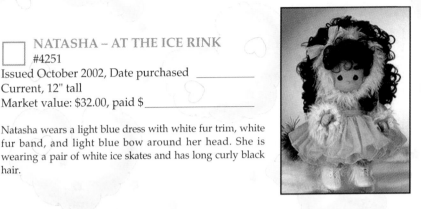

NICOLETTE – AT THE ICE RINK
#4252
Issued October 2002, Date purchased _____
Current, 12" tall
Market value: $38.00, paid $_____

Nicolette is dressed in a light blue outfit with white fur trim, white fur band, and light blue bow around her head. She is wearing a pair of white ice skates and has long curly blond hair.

LOLLIPOP & LAMBSY
#4253
Issued October 2002, Date purchased _____
Current, 12" tall
Market value: $34.00, paid $_____

This cute doll is dressed in a pink velveteen and delicate eyelet lace dress with a matching bonnet. She is carrying her little lamb friend Lambsy. She has long curly blond hair.

KURLER KATHY
#4254

Issued October 2002, Date purchased _____
Current, 12" tall
Market value: $36.00, paid $ _____

Kurler Kathy looks comfortable in her pink house-
coat, pink pajamas, and white bunny slippers. She
has long curly hair with pink hair curlers. She is
carrying her favorite bunny, who is also wearing
pink hair curlers.

MANDY THE MAGICIAN
#4255

Issued October 2002, Date purchased _____
Current, 12" tall
Market value: $36.00, paid $_____

Mandy is ready for her magic act in her black tuxedo and
teal and white polka dot bow. On her head is a matching
black hat with a bunny coming out of it. She has a magic
wand and pink handkerchief in her hands. She has long
curly blond hair. Brenda Miller designed her.

TIPPY TOES BALLERINA
#4256

Issued October 2002, Date purchased _____
Current, 12" tall
Market value: $36.00, paid $_____

Tippy's white ballerina outfit is decorated with ribbons,
pearls, lace, and flowers. She has long curly blond
hair with a white lace band accented with flowers.

GIMME A BEAR HUG

These cute little bears came in three colors: white, grey, and brown. All the bears came with little white bibs with their special sayings: "Gimme A Bear Hug." The bears' inner ears were brown, but some of the bears were produced without inner ears. This was an error.

There are a few folks that received a black bear that were prototypes. These black bears have a secondary market value of $85.00 – 95.00.

☐ **WHITE BEAR**
#1730
Issued 1991, Date purchased _____
Discontinued December 1992, 6" tall
Market value: $30.00 – 35.00 (errored ears, $40.00 – 45.00), paid $_____

☐ **GREY BEAR**
#1731
Issued 1991, Date purchased _____
Discontinued December 1992, 6" tall
Market value: $30.00 – 35.00 (errored ears, $40.00 – 45.00), paid $_____

☐ **BROWN BEAR**
#1732
Issued 1991, Date purchased _____
Discontinued December 1992, 6" tall
Market value: $30.00 – 35.00 (errored ears, $40.00 – 45.00), paid $_____

HI BUNNIES

Precious Moments Bunnies were available in a variety of colors. These adorable characters are sure to touch anyone's heart. All orders placed before Easter 1992 contained additional bibs that read "Hoppy Easter."

Issued 1991
6" tall
Market value: $35.00 – 40.00

□ **PINK BUNNY**
"SOME BUNNY LOVES YOU"
#1701
Date purchased _____
paid $ _____

□ **MINT BUNNY**
"SOME BUNNY LOVES YOU"
#1702
Date purchased _____
paid $ _____

□ **WHITE BUNNY**
"SOME BUNNY LOVES YOU"
#1703
Date purchased _____
paid $ _____

□ **YELLOW BUNNY**
"SOME BUNNY LOVES YOU"
#1704
Date purchased _____
paid $ _____

□ **PEACH BUNNY**
"SOME BUNNY LOVES YOU"
#1705
Date purchased _____
paid $ _____

□ **BLUE BUNNY**
"SOME BUNNY LOVES YOU"
#1706
Date purchased _____
paid $ _____

□ **PINK BUNNY**
"I LOVE YOU"
#1710
Date purchased _____
paid $ _____

□ **PINK BUNNY**
"GET WELL SOON"
#1711
Date purchased _____
paid $ _____

PINK BUNNY
"HOPPY BIRTHDAY"
#1712
Date purchased _____
paid $ _____

BLUE BUNNY
"I LOVE YOU"
#1713
Date purchased _____
paid $ _____

BLUE BUNNY
"GET WELL SOON"
#1714
Date purchased _____
paid $ _____

BLUE BUNNY
"HOPPY BIRTHDAY"
#1715
Date purchased _____
paid $ _____

PEACH BUNNY
"I LOVE YOU"
#1716
Date purchased _____
paid $ _____

PEACH BUNNY
"GET WELL SOON"
#1717
Date purchased _____
paid $ _____

PEACH BUNNY
"HOPPY BIRTHDAY"
#1718
Date purchased _____
paid $ _____

WHITE BUNNY
"I LOVE YOU"
#1719
Date purchased _____
paid $ _____

WHITE BUNNY
"GET WELL SOON"
#1720
Date purchased _____
paid $ _____

WHITE BUNNY
"HOPPY BIRTHDAY"
#1721
Date purchased _____
paid $ _____

HOUSE OF LLOYD EXCLUSIVE

SNUGGLES

Issued 1992, Date purchased _____
Less than 2,000, 16" tall
Market value: $100.00 – 125.00, paid $ _____

Snuggles is dressed in a white bunny outfit. He has blond hair.

SWEETNESS
#4227
Issued October 2002, Date purchased _____
Current, 12" tall
Market value: $36.00, paid $_____

Sweetness is sitting on a cloud wearing a pink angelic outfit with white fur and a white fur halo on her head. She has a pair of white wings on her back.

CHARMED
#4228
Issued October 2002, Date purchased _____
Current, 12" tall
Market value: $36.00, paid $_____

Charmed is sitting on a cloud wearing a blue angelic outfit with white fur and a white fur halo on her head. She has a pair of white wings on her back.

KINDNESS
#4229
Issued October 2002, Date purchased _____
Current, 12" tall
Market value: $36.00, paid $_____

Kindness is sitting on a cloud wearing a blue angelic outfit with white fur and a white fur halo on her head. She has a pair of white wings on her back.

JONATHAN & DAVID

JESUS LOVES ME (GIRL)
#D001
Issued 1984, Date purchased _____
Retired 1988, 14" tall
Market value: $250.00 – 275.00,
paid $ _____

This blond baby girl is dressed in a white
sleeping gown accented at the neckline
with a pink flower.

JESUS LOVES ME (BOY)
#D002
Issued 1984, Date purchased _____
Retired 1988, 14" tall
Market value: $250.00 – 275.00,
paid $ _____

This blond baby boy is dressed in white
pajamas with a blue ribbon at the neckline.

SAILOR SAM
#D004
Issued 1985, Date purchased _____
Retired 1988, 14" – 16" tall
Market value: $250.00 – 275.00,
paid $_____

"The Lord is My Captain" Sam is dressed in
his white navy uniform with a necktie. He
is wearing a white sailor hat on the top of
his head. If found in the original white box,
add $20.00 to the value.

PRIVATE JO JO
#D003
Issued 1985, Date purchased _____
Retired 1988, 14" – 16" tall
Market value: $250.00 – 275.00,
paid $ _____

"I'm in the Lord's Army" Jo Jo is wearing
his army fatigues, boots, and helmet. He has
tan curly hair. If found in the original white
box, add $20.00 to the value.

TOTO
#D005
Issued 1985, Date purchased _____
Retired 1988, 14" tall
Market value: $350.00 – 375.00, paid $ _____

Toto has purple hair with a cone shaped hat. He is wearing a multicolored suit with purple, pink, or white pompoms. The suit is trimmed with white lace, gold rickrack, or yellow floral trim. He is wearing purple shoes.

TAFFY
#D006
Issued 1985, Date purchased _____
Retired 1988, 14" tall
Market value: $325.00 – 350.00, paid $ _____

Taffy is decked in a yellow, blue, and pink striped clown suit with pink pants. She has blond curly hair with a white cap with blue flowers. Her costume is trimmed with lace and her shoes are yellow. She could be found with pink, green, or white pompoms on her top.

PINK MISSY
#D007
Issued 1985, Date purchased _____
Retired 1988, 14" tall
Market value: $250.00 – 275.00, paid $ _____

Missy is wearing a pretty pink satin dress with pleats. She has a white pinafore apron that covers the front of her dress. To identify her, look for the J&D doll tag.

BLUE MISSY
#D008
Issued 1985, Date purchased _____
Retired 1988, 14" tall
Market value: $275.00 – 300.00, paid $ _____

Missy is wearing a pretty blue satin dress with pleats. She has a white pinafore apron that covers the front of her dress. To identify her, look for the J&D doll tag.

PATTI WITH GOOSE
#D009
Issued 1988, Date purchased _____
Retired 1991, 16" tall
Market value: $250.00 – 275.00, paid $ _____

Patti is wearing a pretty rose dress with a white pinafore apron. She has rose ribbons in her hair and comes with a friendly white goose.

LEMSTONE CHRISTIAN BOOKS EXCLUSIVE

Lemstone is the first chain of Christian bookstores to feature a special, limited edition Precious Moments Company doll.

LEAH
#1110
Issued 1997, Date purchased _____
Limited 3,000, 16" tall
Market value: $100.00 – 125.00, paid $ _____

Leah has long blond hair with a red ribbon in it and a beautiful red and white dress. She is carrying a gift box wrapped in gold paper with a red ribbon around it.

☐ FRANCES – SUMMER
#1442
Issued 1999, Date purchased _____
Current, 12" tall
Market value: $34.95, paid $ _____

Frances is dressed for summer in a blue and yellow print dress and a matching blue and yellow hat.

☐ AMIE – SPRING
#1440
Issued 1999, Date purchased _____
Current, 12" tall
Market value: $34.95, paid $ _____

Amie is ready for spring in a light green and white dress with lace trim. She is wearing a white hat on her head with a light green ribbon around it. She is carrying a basket.

☐ TONYA
#1472
Issued 1994, Date purchased _____
1 year production, 12" tall
Market value: $75.00 – 85.00, paid $ _____

Tonya is dressed in a white satin and net dress with pale green panties. She has green ribbons accenting her dress and shoes.

☐ TABITHA – FALL
#1453
Issued 1999, Date purchased _____
Current, 12" tall
Market value: $34.95, paid $ _____

Tabitha's blue denim coveralls and red plaid blouse are a great fall look. She has brown hair with red plaid ribbons in it. She has an apple in her hand.

☐ GLENDA – WINTER
#1452
Issued 1999, Date purchased _____
Current, 12" tall
Market value: $34.95, paid $ _____

Glenda is bundled up for winter in a pink coat with light blue trim and light blue pants. She has a pink and light blue cap, light blue mittens, and white boots on her feet.

LITTLE MISSY
#1473
Issued 1994, Date purchased _____
1 year production, 12" tall
Market value: $75.00 – 85.00, paid $ _____

Missy wears a pink satin dress with a white pinafore. She has long blond hair with pink ribbons in her ponytails.

BECCA
#1474
Issued 1994, Date purchased _____
1 year production, 12" tall
Market value: $75.00 – 85.00, paid $ _____

Becca is dressed in a red satin dress with blue ribbons and ecru lace trim. She has a matching red satin hat on her head.

CHRISTINE
#1476
Issued 1996, Date purchased _____
1 year production, 12" tall
Market value: $75.00 – 85.00, paid $ _____

Christine is clad in a lavender print dress with eyelet lace trim around the sleeves and the underskirt. She is wearing a matching hat on her head. She had a limited run of 4,208 dolls.

CANDIE
#1477
Issued 1996, Date purchased _____
1 year production, 12" tall
Market value: $75.00 – 85.00, paid $ _____

Candie wears a burgundy floral dress with a white satin blouse and black velvet collar. She has black cowboy boots on her feet. She had a limited production of 8,520 dolls.

☐ **LITTLE MARY**
#1495
Issued 1996, Date purchased _____
1 year production, 12" tall
Market value: $75.00 – 85.00, paid $ _____

Mary is dressed in a blue plaid skirt with a green corduroy vest and white blouse. She also has a red tie around her neck. She had a limited production of 7,288 dolls.

MALHAME EXCLUSIVES

☐ **PRAYING CHRISTINA**
#1470
Issued 1997, Date purchased _____
Current, 12" tall
Market value: $34.95, paid $_____

Christina is dressed in a white communion dress with a white veil on her head. She has blond hair.

☐ **PRAYING GRACE**
#1478
Issued 1997, Date purchased _____
Current, 12" tall
Market value: $34.95, paid $_____

Grace is dressed for her First Communion in a white communion dress and white veil. She has pretty brunette hair.

NURSE – AFRICAN-AMERICAN
#1407

Issued 2001, Date purchased _____
Current, 12" tall
Market value: $31.00, paid $_____

This cute little African-American doll is dressed in a white nurse's uniform with matching stockings, shoes, hat, and lab coat. The lab coat can be personalized.

NURSE – CAUCASIAN
#1415B

Issued 2001, Date purchased _____
Current, 12" tall
Market value: $31.00, paid $_____

This cute little blond is dressed in a white nurse's uniform with matching stockings, shoes, hat, and lab coat. The lab coat can be personalized.

MEDICAL PROFESSIONAL – CAUCASIAN
#1481

Issued 2001, Date purchased _____
Suspended 2002, 12" tall
Market value: $31.00, paid $_____

This medical professional wears traditional green scrubs and a white lab coat that can be personalized.

MEDICAL PROFESSIONAL – AFRICAN-AMERICAN
#1489

Issued 2001, Date purchased _____
Current, 12" tall
Market value: $31.00, paid $_____

This medical professional is also wearing traditional green scrubs. His cap can be personalized.

MILITARY SERIES

☐ ARMY GIRL
#1405
Issued 1996, Date purchased _____
Suspended 2001, 12" tall
Market value: $35.00, paid $ _____

This sweet Army Girl is dressed in her green army uniform and hat. She carries a duffel bag.

☐ ARMY BOY
#1406
Issued 1996, Date purchased _____
Suspended 2001, 12" tall
Market value: $35.00, paid $ _____

This cute little Army Boy is wearing his green uniform and hat. He is carrying a duffel bag.

☐ AIR FORCE GIRL
#1408
Issued 1997, Date purchased _____
Suspended January 2001, 12" tall
Market value: $35.00, paid $ _____

Air Force Girl stands at attention in her blue uniform with matching hat. She is carrying a military duffel bag.

☐ AIR FORCE BOY
#1409
Issued 1997, Date purchased _____
Suspended January 2001, 12" tall
Market value: $35.00, paid $ _____

Air Force Boy is handsome in his blue uniform with matching hat. He is carrying a military duffel bag.

NAVY BOY
#1409
Issued 1997, Date purchased _____
Suspended January 2001, 12" tall
Market value: $35.00, paid $ _____

Navy Boy is ready to report in his blue navy uniform with white sailor hat. He is carrying his military duffel bag.

NAVY GIRL
#1410
Issued 1997, Date purchased _____
Suspended January 2001, 12" tall
Market value: $35.00, paid $ _____

Navy Girl wears her blue and white uniform with white and blue hat. She is also carrying a military duffel bag.

MILITARY GIRL IN FATIGUES
#1443
Issued 1997, Date purchased _____
Suspended January 2001, 12" tall
Market value: $35.00, paid $ _____

The girl is wearing a Velcro attached camouflage jacket over her camouflage pants, brown shirt, and matching camouflage cap. She has her dark blond hair pulled up in a knot.

MILITARY BOY IN FATIGUES
#1444
Issued 1997, Date purchased _____
Suspended January 2001, 12" tall
Market value: $35.00, paid $ _____

The boy is wearing a Velcro attached camouflage jacket over his camouflage pants, brown shirt, and matching camouflage cap. He has cropped red hair.

MILITARY GIRL
#1594
Issued 2002, Date purchased _____
Current, 9" tall
Market value: $21.00, paid $_____

The girl is wearing a Velcro attached camouflage jacket over her camouflage pants, brown shirt, and matching camouflage cap. Her dark blond hair is pulled up in a knot.

MILITARY BOY
#1595
Issued 2002, Date purchased _____
Current, 9" tall
Market value: $21.00, paid $_____

The boy is wearing a Velcro attached camouflage jacket over his camouflage pants, brown shirt, and matching camouflage cap. He has cropped red hair.

"MOMMY, I LOVE YOU" SERIES

JANET AND BABY SARAH
#1030
Issued 1992, Date purchased _____
1 year production, 16" tall
Market value: $250.00 – 275.00, paid $_____

This doll was the first edition in the series. Janet has brunette hair that is pulled back in a ponytail and covered with a bonnet that matches her dress. She wears a lavender polka dot dress with an apron. She was named in honor of a very special nanny of the Butcher family that was tragically killed in a motorcycle accident.

JESSI AND BABY LISA
#1044

Issued 1993, Date purchased _____
1 year production, 16" tall
Market value: $200.00 – 225.00, paid $ _____

This doll was the second edition in the series. Jessi has blond hair worn in a high ponytail and has blue eyes. Jessi and Baby Lisa come with a special birth certificate that shows that Lisa is Jessi's and Jonny's new baby girl.

KATHY AND DONNIE
#1060

Issued 1994, Date purchased _____
1 year production, 1994, 16" tall
Market value: $200.00 – 225.00, paid $ _____

Kathy and Donnie are third in the series. Kathy has blond hair worn in two ponytails with a blue scarf wrapped around her head. She wears a work dress with a big white apron. Donnie is dressed in blue and white polka dot pajamas and holds a yellow crayon in his hand with which he drew a sweet picture for his mommy. The picture that Kathy has in her hands says "Mommy you're a princess, you're as sweet as you can be, you're the nicest mom I know, you mean the world to me." Kathy is the only Precious Moments doll that has a molded tear on her cheek.

LORI AND GINNIE
#1082

Issued 1995, Date purchased _____
1 year production, 16" tall
Market value: $175.00 – 200.00, paid $ _____

This doll is the fourth edition in the series. Mommy and her little girl are ready for cooking together. Both dolls have blond hair and blue eyes and are wearing matching light blue checkered pink print dresses and aprons with matching pink shoes.

CARISSA AND BABY TESS
#1088
Issued 1997, Date purchased _____
1 year production, 16" tall
Market value: $80.00 – 100.00, paid $ _____

This doll is the sixth edition in the series. Carissa has long blond hair that is slightly pulled back with pink rose fasteners and is wearing a long pink satin dress with sheer polka dot printed overlay. Baby Tess is dressed in a white satin gown.

SUSAN WITH TWINS
#1101
Issued 1996, Date purchased _____
1 year production, 16" tall
Market value: $150.00 – 175.00, paid $ _____

This doll is the fifth edition in the series. Susan has long blond hair and brown eyes and is carrying two babies dressed in yellow sleepers with sleep caps. Susan is wearing a peach floral print dress with pearl buttons.

KELLY AND ERIN
#1122
Issued 1998, Date purchased _____
1 year production, 16" tall
Market value: $60.00 – 75.00, paid $ _____

Kelly and Erin are seventh in the series. Both have red hair and green eyes. Kelly is wearing a green polka dot dress with a white apron, while Erin is bundled up in a white sleeper.

ANGIE WITH TRIPLETS
#1134
Issued 1999, Date purchased _____
1 year production, 16" tall
Market value: $70.00 – 95.00, paid $ _____

Angie With Triplets is the eighth edition in the series. Angie has long curly blond hair that is pulled up in two ponytails. She is wearing a fun floral print and purple checkered dress. Angie is pushing the triplets in a stroller.

MY ANGEL OF THE RAINBOW

LAVENDER
#4106
Issued October 2002, Date purchased _____
Current, 9" tall
Market value: $29.50, paid $_____

Lavender is dressed in a lavender gown trimmed in lace. She has long straight blond hair with a white halo. She is carrying a white banner that can be personalized.

BLUE
#4107
Issued October 2002, Date purchased _____
Current, 9" tall
Market value: $29.50, paid $_____

Blue wears a light blue gown trimmed in lace. She has long straight brunette hair with a white halo. She is carrying a white banner that can be personalized.

YELLOW
#4108
Issued October 2002, Date purchased _____
Current, 9" tall
Market value: $29.50, paid $_____

Yellow is dressed in a yellow gown trimmed in lace. She has long straight brown hair with a white halo. She is carrying a white banner that can be personalized.

PINK
#4109
Issued October 2002, Date purchased _____
Current, 9" tall
Market value: $29.50, paid $_____

Pink is dressed in a pink gown trimmed in lace. She has long straight blond hair with a white halo. She is carrying a white banner that can be personalized.

GREEN
#4110
Issued October 2002, Date purchased _____
Current, 9" tall
Market value: $29.50, paid $_____

Green is dressed in a light green gown trimmed in lace. She has long straight brown hair with a white halo. She is carrying a white banner that can be personalized.

MY FAVORITE FRIEND SERIES

MAX AND FRIEND
#1309
Issued 1999, Date purchased _____
1 year production, 12" tall
Market value: $29.95, paid $_____

Max is wearing a pair of blue jeans, red and white sneakers, a light blue shirt with a red and blue plaid jacket and a red ball cap on backwards. He is carrying his favorite stuffed friend with him.

KIMMY AND TUBBY
#1416
Issued 1998, Date purchased _____
1 year production, 12" tall
Market value: $69.95, paid $_____

Kimmy is wearing red pajamas complete with sewn-in feet and an old-fashioned buttoned back flap in the bottom with a red plaid robe and red house shoes. Kimmy is carrying an adorable brown teddy bear named Tubby.

MY LITTLE PRINCESS

☐ **CHARMAINE**
#4100
Issued October 2002, Date purchased _____
Current, 9" tall
Market value: $29.50, paid $_____

Charmaine has long curly blond hair with a pink princess crown. She is wearing a pink bridal gown with two full layers of sheer overlay accented with tiny rosebuds.

☐ **CHARLENA**
#4101
Issued October 2002, Date purchased _____
Current, 9" tall
Market value: $29.50, paid $_____

Charlena has long curly brown hair with a white princess crown. She is wearing a white bridal gown with two full layers of sheer overlay accented with tiny rosebuds.

☐ **CHANTEL**
#4102
Issued October 2002, Date purchased _____
Current, 9" tall
Market value: $29.50, paid $_____

Chantel has long curly brown hair with a lavender princess crown. She is wearing a lavender bridal gown with two full layers of sheer overlay accented with tiny rosebuds.

MY WORLD SERIES

☐ **PLAYGROUND SET**
#1662
Date purchased _____
paid $ _____

☐ **ASHLEY (PINK BLANKET)**
#1664
Issued 1999, Date purchased _____
Current, 4" tall
Market value: $12.00, paid $_____

Ashley has blond hair pulled back in two ponytails and has blue eyes. She is wearing a purple and light blue outfit and is carrying a pink blanket.

☐ **BRIAN**
(LAPTOP & GLASSES)
#1665
Issued 1999, Date purchased _____
Current, 4" tall
Market value: $12.00, paid $_____

Brian has blond hair and green eyes. He is wearing black corduroy pants, a green shirt, a plaid jacket, painted on green eyeglasses, and is carrying a black bag that says "laptop."

☐ **CYNDI (TEACHER)**
#1666
Issued 1999, Date purchased _____
Current, 4" tall
Market value: $12.00, paid $ _____

Cyndi has blond hair pulled back in a ponytail and brown eyes. She is wearing a red shirt and a black jumper with alphabet print.

☐ **HANNAH (BUNNY)**
#1667
Issued 1999, Date purchased _____
Current, 4" tall
Market value: $12.00, paid $_____

Hannah has black hair pulled up into ponytails and is wearing a light blue print dress. She is a carrying a lavender bunny.

☐ JONATHAN (FOOTBALL)
#1668
Issued 1999, Date purchased _____
Current, 4" tall
Market value: $12.00, paid $ _____

Jonathan has blond hair and blue eyes. He is wearing a blue leather jacket over a red shirt and blue pants. He is carrying a blue pennant and a football.

☐ NICKY (BLUE BLANKET)
#1670
Issued 1999, Date purchased _____
Current, 4" tall
Market value: $12.00, paid $ _____

Nicky has black hair and brown eyes. She is wearing a blue pair of overalls, a yellow and white striped shirt, and is carrying a light blue blanket.

☐ KAMIE (BASEBALL)
#1669
Issued 1999, Date purchased _____
Current, 4" tall
Market value: $12.00, paid $ _____

Kamie has dark hair pulled back in two long braids and brown eyes. She is wearing a purple shirt with a smiley face on it and a matching purple hat.

☐ SAMANTHA (ROLLER BLADES)
#1671
Issued 1999, Date purchased _____
Current, 4" tall
Market value: $12.00, paid $ _____

Samantha has brown hair pulled back with a pink ribbon. She is wearing light green polka dot coveralls with a yellow polka dot top. She is on a pair of roller blades and has pink kneepads.

NAME YOUR OWN DOLL SERIES

☐ BLOND
#1346
Issued 2000, Date purchased _____
Current, 12" tall
Market value: $31.50, paid $_____

This blond little girl is dressed in a pretty floral dress with a white apron. She has lavender bows in her ponytails. Her apron can be personalized. This doll is a Gocollect.com Exclusive.

BRUNETTE
#1347
Issued 2000, Date purchased _____
Current, 12" tall
Market value: $31.50, paid $_____

Brunette is dressed in a pretty floral dress with a white apron. She has light blue bows in her brunette ponytails. Her apron can be personalized. This doll is a Gocollect.com Exclusive.

ASIAN
#1382
Issued 2001, Date purchased _____
Current, 12" tall
Market value: $31.00, paid $_____

Asian also wears a pretty floral dress with a white apron. She has black hair that is pulled into ponytails. Her apron can be personalized.

CAUCASIAN – BLOND
#1383
Issued 2001, Date purchased _____
Current, 12" tall
Market value: $31.00, paid $_____

This pretty little girl is dressed in a floral dress with a white apron. She has blond hair with a light green ribbon. Her apron can be personalized.

CAUCASIAN – BRUNETTE
#1384
Issued 2001, Date purchased _____
Current, 12" tall
Market value: $31.00, paid $_____

This little brunette is dressed in a floral dress with a white apron.
She has a pink bow in her hair. Her apron can be personalized.

AFRICAN-AMERICAN
#1385
Issued 2001, Date purchased _____
Current, 12" tall
Market value: $31.00, paid $_____

African-American is also dressed in a floral dress with a
white apron. She has black hair with a lavender ribbon.
Her apron can be personalized.

HISPANIC
#1386
Issued 2000, Date purchased _____
Current, 12" tall
Market value: $31.00, paid $_____

This Hispanic doll wears a floral dress with a white apron,
has black hair with a blue bow off the side of her head, and
has an apron that can be personalized.

MORNING STAR WITH PAPOOSE
#1021
Issued 1990, Date purchased _____
Retired 1998, 16" tall
Market value: $125.00 – 150.00, paid $ _____

Morning Star has dark skin, hair worn in two braids, and dark eyes. She is dressed in an authentic-looking brown leather costume. Morning Star has a feather in her headband and is carrying an adorable papoose.

CHIPPEWA
#1401
Issued 1996, Date purchased _____
Limited 5,000, 12" tall
Market value: $59.95, paid $ _____

Chippewa is dressed in her native dress, with a belt around her waist. She has long black braided hair with leather type ribbons in it.

SHOSHONI
#1402
Issued 1996, Date purchased _____
Limited 5,000, 12" tall
Market value: $59.95, paid $_____

Shoshoni is dressed in her native dress, with multicolored accents. She has long black ponytails. She is also wearing a native necklace around her neck.

JICARILLA APACHE
#1403
Issued 1996, Date purchased _____
Limited 5,000, 12" tall
Market value: $59.95, paid $_____

Jicarilla Apache is dressed in her native dress, with a black belt accenting the waistline. She has long black ponytails. She is also wearing a red native necklace.

NAVAJO
#1404
Issued 1996, Date purchased _____
Limited 5,000, 12" tall
Market value: $59.95, paid $_____

Navajo is dressed in a light blue and pink native outfit. She has long black hair pulled into a ponytail. She is also wearing a light blue native necklace.

ZUNI – LOLOTEA
#1482
Issued 1995, Date purchased _____
Limited 7,500, 12" tall
Market value: $59.95, paid $_____

Zuni is dressed in her traditional native outfit with a red scruff on her head, and she is carrying a piece of pottery.

HOPI – YAMKA
#1483
Issued 1995, Date purchased _____
Limited 7,500, 12" tall
Market value: $59.95, paid $_____

Hopi is dressed in her native dress of red and white, with a blue belt accent. She has black ponytails.

YAKIMA – AQUENE
#1484
Issued 1995, Date purchased _____
Limited 7,500, 12" tall
Market value: $59.95, paid $_____

Yakima is dressed in her traditional native outfit with an Indian print around her neck. She is also wearing a native headdress and necklace.

IROQUOIS – LOMASI
#1485
Issued 1995, Date purchased _____
Limited 7,500, 12" tall
Market value: $59.95, paid $_____

Iroquois is dressed in her traditional native outfit with beaded accents. She has long black ponytails. She is also wearing a native necklace.

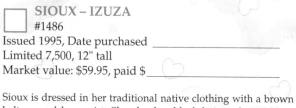

SIOUX – IZUZA
#1486
Issued 1995, Date purchased _____
Limited 7,500, 12" tall
Market value: $59.95, paid $_____

Sioux is dressed in her traditional native clothing with a brown belt around her waist. She also has black hair and a necklace around her neck.

SEMINOLE – AMITOLA
#1487
Issued 1995, Date purchased _____
Limited 7,500, 12" tall
Market value: $59.95, paid $_____

Seminole is dressed in her traditional multicolored native outfit. She has long black hair.

LITTLE SPARROW
#1558
Issued 1998, Date purchased _____
Current, 9" tall
Market value: $21.00, paid $_____

This little doll is dressed in traditional tribal attire. He was the star of his own Precious Moments movie.

NATIVE AMERICAN FAMILY

This cute Native American Family doll set exhibits traditional outfits. These dolls are wonderful additions to any collection.

☐ **WHITE FEATHER WITH LITTLE FEATHER**
#1129
Issued 1998, Date purchased _____
Current, 16" tall
Market value: $79.95, paid $_____

☐ **CHIEF ROARING BEAR**
#1130
Issued 1998, Date purchased _____
Current, 16" tall
Market value: $69.95, paid $_____

☐ **AUTUMN'S LIGHT**
#1451
Issued 1998, Date purchased _____
Current, 12" tall
Market value: $29.95, paid $_____

☐ **SILVER MOON**
#1562
Issued 1998, Date purchased _____
Current, 9" tall
Market value: $21.00, paid $_____

☐ **RUNNING BEAR**
#1639
Issued 1998, Date purchased _____
Current, 7" tall
Market value: $11.00, paid $_____

NATIVITY COLLECTION

☐ **MARY, JOSEPH AND BABY JESUS**
  #1555
Issued 1997, Date purchased _____
Current, 9" tall
Market value: $50.00, paid $_____

Mary is dressed in pink with a lavender shawl. Joseph is dressed in green, blue, and burgundy shepherd's clothing and carries a staff. Jesus is in the crèche.

☐ **NATIVITY SET**
  #1555A
Issued 1997, Date purchased _____
Current
Market value: $90.00 – 95.00, paid $ _____

This nativity starter set includes Mary, Joseph, Jesus, the crèche, and the angel.

☐ **THREE WISE MEN**
  #1561
Issued 1998, Date purchased _____
Current, 9" tall
Market value: $50.00, paid $_____

These three kings are bringing their gifts to the newborn King. They are dressed in ancient robes and have little crowns on their heads.

☐ **LITTLE DRUMMER BOY**
  #1576
Issued 2000, Date purchased _____
Current, 9" tall
Market value: $21.00, paid $_____

Little Drummer Boy wears an ancient outfit and a hat. He is carrying a drum.

SHEPHERD WITH THREE SHEEP
#1593
Issued 2002, Date purchased _____
Current, 9" tall
Market value: $25.00, paid $_____

The Shepherd and his three sheep have come to see the newborn King. He is wearing a green and tan outfit with a sachet around his waist. He is also carrying a shepherd's staff.

NATIVITY ANGEL
#1673
Issued 1999, Date purchased _____
Current, 4" tall
Market value: $6.00, paid $_____

This adorable little angel heralds the birth of Jesus. Dressed in a white angelic gown with gold trim and a pair of wings on her back, she makes a perfect addition to your nativity scene.

NATIVITY CRÈCHE
#1674
Issued 1999, Date purchased _____
Current, 12" tall
Market value: $25.00, paid $_____

This crèche is the perfect setting in which to display the beautiful nativity scene.

NURSERY RHYMES SERIES

☐ **GOLDILOCKS**
#1303
Issued 1999, Date purchased _____
Current, 12" tall
Market value: $29.50, paid $_____

Goldilicks is the fourth edition in the Nursery Rhymes Series.
She has dark blond hair and is wearing a white and red dress.
She is carrying a cute little teddy bear.

☐ **LITTLE BO PEEP**
#1316
Issued 2001, Date purchased _____
Current, 12" tall
Market value: $29.50, paid $_____

Little Bo Peep is the seventh edition in the Nursery Rhymes
Series. She has blond hair pulled back under her bonnet and
blue eyes. She holds one of her little lambs with a yellow leash.

☐ **MOTHER GOOSE**
#1330
Issued 2000, Date purchased _____
Current, 12" tall
Market value: $29.50, paid $_____

Mother Goose is the fifth edition in the Nursery Rhymes
Series. She comes with a pair of eyeglasses and is dressed
in a white, blue, and yellow dress with a matching bonnet.
She has her pet goose on a ribbon leash.

☐ **MARY, MARY, QUITE CONTRARY**
#1349
Issued 2000, Date purchased _____
Current, 12" tall
Market value: $29.50, paid $_____

Mary is the sixth edition in the Nursery Rhymes Series. She
has strawberry red hair, green eyes, and is dressed in a green
checkered and floral print dress. She is carrying a watering can
and a garden spade. She also has a straw hat on her head.

LITTLE MISS MUFFET
#1418
Issued 1998, Date purchased _____
Current, 12" tall
Market value: $29.50, paid $_____

Little Miss Muffet is the third editon in the Nursery Rhymes Series. She wears a pretty outfit trimmed in pink and is carrying a bowl and spoon. She has blond hair with bangs and is adorable. Not only is a little spider sitting beside her, it sits on her shoulder.

LITTLE RED RIDING HOOD
#1419
Issued 1998, Date purchased _____
Current, 12" tall
Market value: $29.50, paid $_____

Little Red Riding Hood is the first edition in the Nursery Rhymes Series. She is wearing a blue and white checkered dress, a red cape with hood, and is carrying a basket. She has wavy brown hair with bangs and blue eyes. There were a few brunettes produced with blue eyes.

MARY HAD A LITTLE LAMB
#1420
Issued 1998, Date purchased _____
Current, 12" tall
Market value: $29.50, paid $_____

Mary is the second edition in the Nursery Rhymes Series. She has long dark blond braids and is wearing a blue denim dress. She is carrying a shepherd's staff and has her little lamb with her.

"PEARLS & LACE" SERIES

VICTORIA
#1115
Issued July 1997, Date purchased _____
Limited 3,500, 16" tall
Market value: $69.95, paid $_____

Victoria is wearing a mint green gown accented with pearls and lace. She was named in honor of Vicki Cash, the editor of *Chapel Bells Magazine*.

PLAID RAG DOLLS COLLECTION

GREEN & PINK PLAID
#1610
Issued 1995, Date purchased _____
Discontinued 1996, 7" tall
Market value: $25.00 – 30.00, paid $ _____

Green & Pink Plaid is wearing a green and pink plaid skirt and vest with a white blouse. She has a plaid heart tied to her vest. Her hair is yellow with a plaid headband.

RED & BLUE PLAID
#1611
Issued 1995, Date purchased _____
Discontinued 1996, 7" tall
Market value: $25.00 – 30.00, paid $ _____

Red & Blue Plaid is wearing a blue and red plaid romper. She has yellow hair with blue satin bows and a plaid beret. She has two hearts decorating her romper.

BLUE & YELLOW PLAID
#1612
Issued 1995, Date purchased _____
Discontinued 1996, 7" tall
Market value: $25.00 – 30.00, paid $ _____

Blue & Yellow Plaid is wearing a powder blue, pink, and white pinafore with a white blouse and skirt trimmed in lace. She has a red, yellow, and black plaid heart on her dress.

ROYAL BLUE PLAID
#1613
Issued 1995, Date purchased _____
Discontinued 1996, 7" tall
Market value: $25.00 – 30.00, paid $ _____

Royal Blue Plaid is wearing a royal blue plaid skirt with a white blouse trimmed with lace. She has blond hair tied with green satin ribbons into braids. She has a red plaid heart around her neck.

PLUSH ANIMALS

☐ **SIMON THE LAMB (BLUE)**
   #1725
Issued 1995, Date purchased _____
Discontinued 1997, 4" tall
Market value: $22.00 – 25.00, paid $ _____

This cute little blue lamb is from the Precious Moments
movie "Simon the Lamb."

☐ **SIMON THE LAMB (WHITE)**
   #1726
Issued 1995, Date purchased _____
Discontinued 1996, 4" tall
Market value: $22.00 – 25.00, paid $ _____

This cute little white lamb is from the Precious Moments
movie "Simon the Lamb."

Charlie Bear came in four different sizes. He is brown with a tuft of tan hair
on top of his head and a little tan tail. He has a large red bow around his neck.

☐ **CHARLIE BEAR**
   #1742
Issued 1994, Date purchased _____
Discontinued 1998, 15" tall
Market value: $20.00 – 25.00, paid $ _____

☐ **CHARLIE BEAR**
   #1743
Issued 1994, Date purchased _____
Discontinued 1998, 21" tall
Market value: $37.00 – 45.00, paid $ _____

CHARLIE BEAR
☐ #1744
Issued 1994, Date purchased _____
Discontinued 1998, 48" tall
Market value: $300.00 – 325.00, paid $ _____

CHARLIE BEAR
☐ #1748
Issued 1994, Date purchased _____
Discontinued 1994, 9" tall
Market value: $12.00 – 17.00, paid $ _____

SNOWBALL BEAR
☐ #1745
Issued 1994, Date purchased _____
Discontinued 1996, 15" tall
Market value: $50.00 – 75.00, paid $ _____

Snowball has white fur, green eyes, and a simple red ribbon around his neck. He also has a red Precious Moments emblem embroidered on his behind.

BABY'S FIRST BEAR (BLUE)
☐ #1746
Issued 1994, Date purchased _____
Discontinued 1996, 9" tall
Market value: $35.00 – 45.00, paid $ _____

BABY'S FIRST BEAR (PINK)
☐ #1747
Issued 1994, Date purchased _____
Discontinued 1996, 9" tall
Market value: $35.00 – 45.00, paid $ _____

BABY'S FIRST BEAR (BROWN)
☐ #1748
Issued 1994, Date purchased _____
Discontinued 1996, 9" tall
Market value: $35.00 – 45.00, paid $ _____

Each Baby's First Bear has a sewn-in bellybutton, sewn teardrop eyes, and a white plastic Precious Moments tag. They come in blue, pink, or brown and each has a ribbon around its neck with its name on it — "Baby's First Bear."

GROOM BEAR
#1750
Issued 1995, Date purchased _____
Discontinued 1998, 15" tall
Market value: $35.00 – 50.00,
paid $ _____

Groom Bear is brown with a black tuxedo hat on his head. Around his neck is a white collar with a black bow tie, and around his wrists are white cuffs.

BRIDE BEAR
#1749
Issued 1995, Date purchased _____
Discontinued 1998, 15" tall
Market value: $35.00 – 50.00,
paid $ _____

Bride Bear is white with a sheer lace veil on her head. She is carrying a little bouquet of flowers.

CUPID BEAR
#1751
Issued 1995, Date purchased _____
Discontinued 1995, 16" tall
Market value: $100.00 – 150.00, paid $ _____

Cupid Bear is white and carries a white satin bag of arrows and a bow. He has a halo on his head. This bear was never released to retailers. The first shipment did not meet the PMC specifications, so the bear was never produced for retail sales. There are some available on the secondary market.

SNOWBALL BEAR WITH VEST
#1757
Issued 1995, Date purchased _____
Discontinued 1996, 15" tall
Market value: $35.00 – 50.00, paid $ _____

Snowball has white fur, green eyes, and a simple red ribbon around his neck. He is dressed in a red and green plaid vest with a red satin ribbon. This bear also has a red Precious Moments emblem embroidered on his behind.

BAILEY BUNNY
#1758
Issued 1996, Date purchased _____
Suspended January 2001, 15" tall
Market value: $21.95, paid $_____

Bailey has a pink bellybutton and nose and pink satin inside her ears and on the pads of her feet. The Precious Moments logo is embroidered on her feet and a pretty pink bow is tied around her neck.

PARKER PLAID BEAR
#1760
Issued 1996, Date purchased _____
Discontinued 1998, 12" tall
Market value: $29.95, paid $_____

Parker is jointed together with buttons and constructed with plaid fabrics. The Precious Moments Logo is embroidered on his right foot.

DILLON DENIM BEAR
#1761
Issued 1996, Date purchased _____
Discontinued 1998, 12" tall
Market value: $29.95, paid $_____

Dillon is jointed together with buttons and constructed with denim. The Precious Moments Logo is embroidered on his right foot.

COLTON CORDUROY BEAR
#1762
Issued 1996, Date purchased _____
Discontinued 1998, 12" tall
Market value: $29.95, paid $_____

Colton is jointed together with buttons and constructed with corduroy. The Precious Moments Logo is embroidered on his right foot.

☐ **LANDON BEAR**
   #1763
Issued 1996, Date purchased _____
Discontinued 1998, 15" tall
Market value: $29.95, paid $_____

Landon & Letty (below) have grayish fur, sewn-on bellybuttons and eyebrows, teardrop eyes, and red patches of the Precious Moments logo sewn on their right feet. Landon is wearing a blue plaid bow tie and Letty wears a red corduroy dress with a matching bow in front of her ear.

☐ **LETTY BEAR**
   #1764
Issued 1996, Date purchased _____
Discontinued 1998, 15" tall
Market value: $29.95, paid $_____

Edmond & Eyvette have tan fur, sewn-on bellybuttons and eyebrows, teardrop eyes, and red patches of the Precious Moments logo sewn on their right feet. Edmond is wearing a blue plaid vest and bow tie and Evyette wears a blue corduroy dress with a matching bow in front of her ear.

☐ **EDMOND BEAR**
   #1765
Issued 1996, Date purchased _____
Discontinued 1998, 15" tall
Market value: $29.95, paid $_____

☐ **EYVETTE BEAR**
   #1766
Issued 1996, Date purchased _____
Discontinued 1998, 15" tall
Market value: $29.95, paid $_____

TREVOR BEAR (RED SWEATER)
#1767
Issued 1997, Date purchased _____
Suspended 1999, 21" tall
Market value: $45.00 – 50.00, paid $ _____

Trevor is a gray colored bear with white tips on his fur. He is wearing a red winter sweater with a red and white scarf.

BAXTER BEAR (BLUE SWEATER)
#1768
Issued 1997, Date purchased _____
Suspended 1999, 21" tall
Market value: $45.00 – 50.00, paid $ _____

Baxter is a tan colored bear with white tips on his fur. He is wearing a blue winter sweater with a blue and white scarf.

GRANT BEAR IN STOCKING
#1769
Issued 1996, Date purchased _____
Discontinued 1998, 15" tall
Market value: $29.95, paid $ _____

Grant Bear has gray fur and comes in a red stocking.

CHRIS BEAR IN STOCKING
#1770
Issued 1996, Date purchased _____
Discontinued 1998, 11" tall
Market value: $29.95, paid $ _____

Chris Bear has white fur and comes in a red plush stocking that's ready to hang.

PRECIOUS COLLECTION

☐ **CHLOE**
☐ #1260
Issued 2001, Date purchased _____
Limited 500, 16" tall
Market value: $179.95, paid $_____

Southern Belle Chloe is wearing a floral dress with a matching bow in her beautiful blond bobbed hair. She is carrying a soft teddy bear.

☐ **COURTNEY**
☐ #1261
Issued 2001, Date purchased _____
Limited 500, 16" tall
Market value: $69.95, paid $_____

"Charming with Delight" Courtney is a gorgeous redhead. She has brown eyes, beautiful brown curly hair, and is carrying a soft teddy bear. She is dressed in a long blue print dress trimmed with lace and has a matching hat.

☐ **DEBBI**
☐ #1262
Issued 2001, Date purchased _____
Limited 500, 16" tall
Market value: $89.95, paid $_____

"Puppies by the Pound" Debbi is dressed in a long brown dog print and white-laced dress with a matching hat. She is carrying a little brown dog.

☐ **DANIEL**
☐ #1263
Issued 2001, Date purchased _____
Limited 500, 16" tall
Market value: $89.95, paid $_____

"Puppies by the Pound" Daniel is dressed in a brown dog print and white outfit with a matching hat. He is carrying a little brown dog.

THE LITTLEST ANGEL
#1264
Issued 2001, Date purchased _____
Limited 500, 16" tall
Market value: $239.95, paid $_____

The Littlest Angel is dressed in a beautiful long white gown with rose accents and has a matching hat on her head. She has long curly blond hair.

LAYLEE
#1265
Issued 2001, Date purchased _____
Limited 500, 16" tall
Market value: $179.95, paid $_____

"Ladybug Lane" Laylee has blond hair with red ribbons in her ponytails. She is wearing a pair of red glasses and a long blue ladybug print dress.

THE FAIRY PRINCESS
#1266
Issued 2001, Date purchased _____
Limited 500, 16" tall
Market value: $239.95, paid $_____

The Fairy Princess wears a beautiful pink satin gown with a large pink hat. She has long curly blond hair.

GABBY THE GLAMOUR GIRL
#1267
Issued 2001, Date purchased _____
Limited 500, 16" tall
Market value: $99.95, paid $_____

Gabby is an adorable blond playing "dress up." She has fake eyelashes, painted fingernails, a ring, purse, feather boa, and lipstick that she has applied a little crooked.

GABBY THE GLAMOUR GIRL
#1268
Issued 2001, Date purchased _____
Limited 500, 26" tall
Market value: $199.95, paid $_____

Gabby is an adorable blond playing "dress up." She has fake eyelashes, painted fingernails, a ring, purse, feather boa, and lipstick just like 16" Gabby on the previous page.

FAIRY OF PROMISE
#1269
Issued 2001, Date purchased _____
Limited 1,000, 7" tall
Market value: $22.00, paid $_____

Fairy of Promise has beautiful curly blond hair with pink flowers. She is dressed in a pink lace dress with pink flowers and has a pink ribbon around her left ankle.

FAIRY OF LOVE
#1270
Issued 2001, Date purchased _____
Limited 1,000, 7" tall
Market value: $22.00, paid $_____

Fairy of Love has beautiful curly brown hair with lavender flowers. She is dressed in a lavender lace dress with lavender flowers and has a lavender ribbon around her left ankle.

FAIRY OF HAPPINESS
#1271
Issued 2002, Date purchased _____
Limited 2,500, 7" tall
Market value: $25.00, paid $_____

Fairy of Happiness has beautiful curly blond hair with green flowers. She is dressed in a green lace dress with green flowers and has a green ribbon around her left ankle.

FAIRY OF FRIENDSHIP
#1272
Issued 2002, Date purchased _____
Limited 2,500, 7" tall
Market value: $25.00, paid $_____

Fairy of Friendship has beautiful curly brown hair with yellow flowers. She is dressed in a yellow lace dress with yellow flowers and has a yellow ribbon around her left ankle.

HEAVEN'S MAJESTY
#1273
Issued 2002, Date purchased _____
Numbered Edition, 16" tall
Market value: $99.95, paid $ _____

Heaven's Majesty is dressed in a pink satin gown. She has long curly blond hair with a jeweled halo. On her back is a set of real feather wings.

STACEY
#1274
Issued 2002, Date purchased _____
Limited 2,500, 16" tall
Market value: $100.00, paid $_____

Stacey has striking dark brown hair with a feather band. She is wearing an ivory bridal satin gown with floral trim. She has beautiful white feather wings on her back.

ALEXANDRA
#1275
Issued 2002, Date purchased _____
Limited 2,500, 16" tall
Market value: $100.00, paid $ _____

Alexandra is stunning in her green bridal satin gown that highlights her auburn hair and green eyes. She has white wings on her back.

BEDTIME BRENDA
#1276
Issued 2002, Date purchased _____
Limited 2,500, 16" tall
Market value: $100.00, paid $_____

Brenda is all ready for bed in her adorable pink nightgown adorned with five little sheep and accented with ivory marabou. Doll was designed by Brenda Miller.

BERRY SWEET
#1277
Issued 2002, Date purchased _____
Limited 2,500, 16" tall
Market value: $100.00, paid $_____

Berry comes in a white dress with red strawberries and green leaves. She has blond hair with red ribbons. She is carrying a basket of strawberries.

CLEMENTINE & HER CLOTHESLINE
#1278
Issued 2002, Date purchased _____
Limited 1,500, 16" tall
Market value: $90.00, paid $_____

Clementine is dressed in a pretty cream dress with lace trim around her neckline. She is carrying her clothesline with her favorite bunnies. She has red hair with clothespins in it.

CLARA & BELLE
#1279
Issued 2002, Date purchased _____
Limited 1,500, 16" tall
Market value: $100.00, paid $_____

Clara comes with her friend Belle the cow. She is dressed in a green and white farm print pinafore. Clara has long black hair in braids with red ribbons. She also comes with a milk pail.

SIERRA
#1280
Issued 2002, Date purchased _____
Limited 2,500, 16" tall
Market value: $110.00, paid $_____

Sierra is dressed in a white lace and satin dress. She
has blond hair with a white feather band. On her back
is a pair of white feather wings.

BRIANNA
#1281
Issued 2002, Date purchased _____
Limited 2,500, 16" tall
Market value: $100.00, paid $_____

Brianna is a princess clothed in a light blue satin dress
accented with flowers. She has long blond hair with a
blue crown. She is carrying a pretty staff.

KAITLYN & KIRBY
#1282
Issued 2002, Date purchased _____
Limited 1,500, 16" tall
Market value: $100.00, paid $_____

Kaitlyn comes with her favorite friend Kirby, a fluffy
white dog. Kaitlyn is dressed in a green outfit with
white fur trim. She has a matching hat on her head
and long blond hair.

"PRECIOUS JEWELS" SERIES

☐ **DESERT ROSE**
#1221
Issued 1996, Date purchased _____
1 year production, 18" tall
Market value: $200.00, paid $ _____

Desert Rose is a Native American doll with long black hair with a leather band and feather on her head. She is dressed in her native leather beaded gown.

☐ **JADE**
#1222
Issued 1996, Date purchased _____
1 year production, 18" tall
Market value: $200.00, paid $ _____

Jade is a lovely Oriental doll wearing a long teal Oriental gown. She has pretty black hair and brown eyes.

☐ **PEARL**
#1223
Issued 1996, Date purchased _____
1 year production, 18" tall
Market value: $200.00, paid $ _____

Pearl has short curly blond hair and blue eyes. She is wearing a long white satin gown.

☐ **BERYL**
#1224
Issued 1996, Date purchased _____
1 year production, 18" tall
Market value: $200.00, paid $ _____

Beryl is a lovely doll with a long yellow gown. She has long light brown hair with a yellow ribbon in it and green eyes.

RUBY
#1225
Issued 1996, Date purchased _____
1 year production, 18" tall
Market value: $200.00, paid $_____

Ruby is a gorgeous brunette doll wearing a long red gown with a matching hat. She has brown eyes.

AMBER
#1226
Issued 1996, Date purchased _____
1 year production, 18" tall
Market value: $200.00, paid $_____

Amber has long curly auburn hair and brown eyes. She is wearing a long amber dress.

SAPPHIRE
#1227
Issued 1996, Date purchased _____
1 year production, 18" tall
Market value: $200.00, paid $_____

Sapphire is an elegant doll with pretty brunette hair with a dark blue bow in it. She is wearing a long dark blue gown.

☐ **CRYSTAL**
#1228
Issued 1996, Date purchased _____
1 year production, 18" tall
Market value: $200.00, paid $_____

Crystal has long straight blond hair and blue eyes. She is wearing a long beautiful white gown and has a white bow on her head.

☐ **OPAL**
#1229
Issued 1996, Date purchased _____
1 year production, 18" tall
Market value: $200.00, paid $_____

Opal is a pretty doll with short curly blond hair and blue eyes. She is wearing a long opalescent pink gown.

☐ **JASPER**
#1230
Issued 1996, Date purchased _____
1 year production, 18" tall
Market value: $200.00, paid $_____

Jasper is an elegant doll with long brunette hair with a maroon bow in it and has brown eyes. She is wearing a long maroon/wine colored gown.

The Preciousmomentscommunity.com website is a site for Precious Moments collectors to join an online club with a lot of information, contests, chat room, and much more.

GRETCHEN – GERMANY
Issued 1997, Retired December 2, 1998
Limited 2, 16" tall

Gretchen is a 16" soft body version of Gretchen (Germany) in the Children of the World Series. She was created especially for The Precious Moments Community website and is in the Gallery of the Precious Moments Chapel.

ALLISON – AMERICA
Issued 1997, Retired December 2, 1999
Limited 2, 16" tall

Allison is a 16" soft body version of Allison (USA) in the Children of the World Series. She was created for the Precious Moments Community website and is in the Gallery of the Precious Moments Chapel.

CAITLYN – IRELAND
Issued 1999, Retired December 31, 2000
Limited 2, 16" tall

Caitlyn is a 16" version of Caitlyn (Ireland) from the Children of the World Series. She was created especially for the Precious Moments Community website.

SULU – ALASKA
Issued 2000, Retired December 2001
Limited 2, 16" tall

Sulu is a 16" version of the Sulu (Alaska) from the Children of the World Series. She was created especially for the Precious Moments Community website and is in the Gallery of the Precious Moments Chapel.

MEG O' BYTE
Issued 2001, Current
13" tall

Meg comes with a laptop and a stool. She has the PM logo on the front of her jacket and angels on the back. She has the Precious Moments Community logo on the screen of her laptop. Meg is the first in a series that is completely exclusive to the website.

GLITCHEN
Issued 2002, Current
13" tall

Glitchen comes with a laptop and a stool. She is wearing a traditional German outfit in red with a white apron. She wears a black German hat. Glitchen is the second in a series that is completely exclusive to the Precious Moments Community website.

MEI LING WITH LING LING
Issued 2002, Limited Edition
17" tall

Mei Ling is dressed in a green and white Chinese outfit with a straw hat on her head. She is with her friend Ling Ling the panda. This doll is the sixth edition in the series created exclusively for the Precious Moments Community website.

BELLA WITH DIEGO
Issued 2002, Limited Edition
17" tall

Bella is dressed in a multicolored and white trimmed Mexican dress and comes with her friend Diego the horse. She was the seventh edition in the series created exclusively for the Precious Moments Community website.

COLIN THE MOUSE
#1794
Issued 1998, Date purchased _____
Limited 3,000, 6" tall
Market value: $30.00 – 45.00, paid $_____

Colin was an exclusive to the Precious Moments Collectible Treasures Website (now Precious Moments Community). This little gray mouse is holding a piece of cheese.

PRECIOUS MOMENTS COMPANY PROMOTION EXCLUSIVE

NINA
Issued 1993, Date purchased _____
Limited 30, 16" tall
Market value: $1,300.00 – 1,500.00, paid $ _____

Nina has brunette hair and is wearing a rosebud print dress. The Precious Moments Company included an offer to register for a drawing for this special doll. There were 30 dolls awarded to 30 doll collectors.

PRECIOUS PALS COLLECTION

Precious Pals are the original Precious Moments Company's "beanie-type" stuffed animals. What makes these little guys so special is that each pal represents a different character in one of the Precious Moments' cartoon videos.

Simon the Lamb – from *Simon the Lamb*
Snowball the Bunny – from *Timmy's Gift*
Jeremy the Toucan – from *Who's Who at the Zoo*
Georgina the Giraffe – from *Who's Who at the Zoo*
Dudley the Dog – from *Timmy's Special Delivery*
Hopper the Sparrow – from *Little Sparrow*

GEORGINA THE GIRAFFE #1734 Issued 1997, Date purchased _____ Retired 1998, 6" tall Market value: $7.00, paid $ _____	**JEREMY THE TOUCAN** #1735 Issued 1997, Date purchased _____ Retired 1998, 6" tall Market value: $7.00, paid $ _____
HOPPER THE SPARROW #1736 Issued 1997, Date purchased _____ Retired 1998, 6" tall Market value: $7.00, paid $ _____	**SIMON THE LAMB** #1737 Issued 1997, Date purchased _____ Retired 1998, 6" tall Market value: $7.00, paid $ _____
DUDLEY THE DOG #1738 Issued 1997, Date purchased _____ Retired 1998, 6" tall Market value: $7.00, paid $ _____	**SNOWBALL THE BUNNY** #1739 Issued 1997, Date purchased _____ Retired 1998, 6" tall Market value: $7.00, paid $ _____

These Precious Pals are the second editions in the series. These pals also come from the Precious Moments cartoon videos.

Teacher the Goose – from *Simon the Lamb*
Buzz the Bee – from *Little Sparrow*
Thor the Dog – from *Timmy's Special Delivery*

Alek the Lion – from *Who's Who at the Zoo*
Nicodemus the Pig – from *Timmy's Gift*
Jacob the Cat – from *Timmy's Special Delivery*

☐ **TEACHER THE GOOSE**
#1788
Issued 1998, Date purchased _____
Retired 1999, 6" tall
Market value: $6.00, paid $_____

☐ **BUZZ THE BEE**
#1789
Issued 1998,
Date purchased _____
Retired 1999, 6" tall
Market value: $6.00,
paid $ _____

☐ **THOR THE DOG**
#1790
Issued 1998, Date purchased _____
Retired 1999, 6" tall
Market value: $6.00, paid $_____

☐ **ALEK THE LION**
#1791
Issued 1998, Date purchased _____
Retired 1999, 6" tall
Market value: $6.00, paid $ _____

☐ **NICODEMUS THE PIG**
#1792
Issued 1998, Date purchased _____
Retired 1999, 6" tall
Market value: $6.00, paid $_____

JACOB THE CAT
#1793
Issued 1998, Date purchased _____
Retired 1999, 6" tall
Market value: $6.00, paid $_____

These pals are the third editions in the series. These pals also come from the Precious Moments cartoon videos.

Shep the Sheep Dog – from *Simon the Lamb*   Renny the Rhino – from *Who's Who at the Zoo*
Ellie the Elephant – from *Who's Who at the Zoo*   Titus the Squirrel – from *Timmy's Gift*
Bernard the Bear – from *Little Sparrow*   Daisy the Lamb – from *Simon the Lamb*

SHEP THE SHEEP DOG
#1773
Issued 1999, Date purchased _____
Current, 6" tall
Market value: $7.00, paid $ _____

RENNY THE RHINO
#1776
Issued 1999, Date purchased _____
Current, 6" tall
Market value: $7.00, paid $ _____

ELLIE THE ELEPHANT
#1774
Issued 1999, Date purchased _____
Current, 6" tall
Market value: $7.00, paid $ _____

TITUS THE SQUIRREL
#1777
Issued 1999, Date purchased _____
Current, 6" tall
Market value: $7.00, paid $ _____

BERNARD THE BEAR
#1775
Issued 1999, Date purchased _____
Current, 6" tall
Market value: $7.00, paid $ _____

DAISY THE LAMB
#1778
Issued 1999, Date purchased _____
Current, 6" tall
Market value: $7.00, paid $ _____

☐ GIL THE FISH

Issued 1997, Date purchased _____
Limited 1,750, 5" tall
Market value: $25.00, paid $_____

Gil was a gift to Precious Moments Collectors who
attended the third annual Licensee Show (1997) at the
Precious Moments Chapel.

☐ CLUCK THE ROOSTER

Issued 1998, Date purchased _____
Limited 1,500, 5" tall
Market value: $25.00, paid $_____

Cluck was a Gift to Precious Moments Collectors who
attended the fourth annual Licensee Show (1998) at the Precious Moments Chapel.

☐ CHIRP THE BIRD

Issued 1999, Date purchased _____
Limited 1,500, 5" tall
Market value: $25.00, paid $_____

Chirp was a gift to Precious Moments Collectors who attended
the fifth annual Licensee Show (1999) at the Precious
Moments Chapel.

PRECIOUS PLAYERS COLLECTION

TINA – TENNIS
#1629

Issued 1996, Date purchased _____

Current, 11" tall

Market value: $8.00, paid $ _____

Tina is dressed for a day of tennis in a red and white outfit. She has yellow hair with a red ribbon and is carrying a tennis racket.

GORDON – GOLF
#1630

Issued 1996, Date purchased _____

Current, 11" tall

Market value: $8.00, paid $ _____

Gordon is ready for a game of golf in his gray polo shirt and plaid pants. He has a blue hat covering his black hair and is carrying a golf club.

BENSON – BASKETBALL
#1631

Issued 1996, Date purchased _____

Current, 11" tall

Market value: $8.00, paid $ _____

Benson is ready to shoot some hoops in his yellow sweatsuit. He has black hair and is carrying a basketball.

SADIE – SOFTBALL
#1632

Issued 1996, Date purchased _____

Current, 11" tall

Market value: $8.00, paid $ _____

Sadie is ready to play ball in her white top trimmed in pink and a pair of pink and white striped pants. She has blond hair with pink ribbons and is carrying a baseball bat.

FLINT – FOOTBALL
#1633
Issued 1996, Date purchased _____
Current, 11" tall
Market value: $8.00, paid $_____

Flint is ready for a touchdown in his green uniform with yellow trim. He has blond hair and is carrying a football.

CASSIE – CHEERLEADER
#1634
Issued 1996, Date purchased _____
Current, 11" tall
Market value: $8.00, paid $_____

Cassie is ready to cheer in her red and white cheerleading uniform. She has blond hair with red ribbons in her ponytails.

SYDNEY – SOCCER
#1635
Issued 1996, Date purchased _____
Current, 11" tall
Market value: $8.00, paid $_____

Sydney is ready for a game of soccer in her black uniform with yellow trim. She has black hair with a yellow ribbon and is carrying a soccer ball.

HANSFORD – HOCKEY
#1636
Issued 1996, Date purchased _____
Current, 11" tall
Market value: $8.00, paid $_____

Hansford is ready for a game of hockey in his white uniform with red, white, and blue trim. He has blond hair and is carrying a hockey stick.

PREFERRED DOLL RETAILER

Preferred Doll Retailers are stores which the Precious Moments Company has selected as their top accounts. Stores with a Preferred Doll Retailer (PDR) account have the opportunity to sell these dolls created exclusively for their stores.

☐ **AMY**
#1034
Issued 1992, Date purchased _____
Limited 4,000, 16" tall
Market value: $200.00 – 225.00, paid $ _____

Amy is dressed in a pink floral print dress with blue and white pinafore. She has large blue bows on her braids. She is carrying a framed message, "Precious Moments never end when shared with my forever friend."

☐ **CARLA**
#1036
Issued 1994, Date purchased _____
1 year production, 16" tall
Market value: $175.00 – 200.00, paid $ _____

Carla is dressed in a pastel floral blouse and lavender and pink shirt. She has blond hair with pretty bows and is carrying a yellow and blue jar of cookies.

☐ **CARA**
#1045
Issued 1993, Date purchased _____
Suspended, 16" tall
Market value: $175.00 – 200.00, paid $ _____

Cara is dressed in a pink and green floral dress accented with pink ruffles at the wrists and hem. She also has a pink collar. The doll was recalled due to a "bad hair day." She has a little cart with her favorite friend in it.

LITTLE SUNSHINE
#1051
Issued 1996, Date purchased _____
Limited 5,000, 16" tall
Market value: $75.00 – 100.00, paid $ _____

Little Sunshine is dressed in a black and white checkered dress with eyelet lace. On her dress, shoes, and headband are little sunflowers.

ROBYN
#1081
Issued 1995, Date purchased _____
1 year production, 16" tall
Market value: $75.00 – 100.00, paid $ _____

Robyn is dressed in a blue and pink floral coat with blue and pink plaid pants. She is wearing a big pink hat with a big blue silk flower on her head.

LACEY
#1106
Issued 1997, Date purchased _____
Limited 3,500, 16" tall
Market value: $55.00 – 75.00, paid $ _____

Lacey is dressed in a rose printed dress with mauve and white lace trim on the lower skirt accented with pink satin ribbons. She has a pink ribbon in her hair.

MARY JO
#1325
Issued 1999, Date purchased _____
1 year production, 12" tall
Market value: $29.95, paid $ _____

Mary Jo is wearing purple checkered pants with a matching hat and roller skates and carries a tray with a shake and a burger. She has medium blond hair that is flipped up at the bottom and has brown eyes. She is the second edition in the Nostalgic Series.

BETTY LOU
#1365
Issued 2001, Date purchased _____
1 year production, 12" tall
Market value: $29.95, paid $_____

Betty Lou has dark blond hair in two ponytails, brown eyes, and plays with a hula-hoop. She is wearing red and white checkered pants with a blue sweater with the letter "P" on it. She is the third edition in the Nostalgic Series.

PEGGY SUE
#1413
Issued 1998, Date purchased _____
1 year production, 12" tall
Market value: $75.00 – 100.00, paid $ _____

Peggy Sue's long blond hair is pulled back in a ponytail with a pink scarf. She wears black and white saddle oxfords, a pink "Letter" jacket with a "P" emblem, and a pink poodle skirt complete with a chain on the poodle. She is the first edition in the Nostalgic Series.

SARA AND KARA
#1445
Issued 1997, Date purchased _____
1 year production, 12" tall
Market value: $79.95, paid $ _____

Sara and Kara each have brown hair and brown eyes, wear matching light denim outfits, and a half of a heart - shaped necklace that reads "Sisters' and Friends' Love Never Ends" when put together.

AMORE
#1600
Issued 1999, Date purchased _____
Limited 1,500, 26" tall
Market value: $129.95, paid $_____

Amore has purple yarn hair and is wearing a lavender, pink, yellow, and green satin print outfit with matching jester hat and shoes.

☐ **SUNSHINE**
   #1605
Issued 1994, Date purchased _____
Limited 450, 26" tall
Market value: $1,000.00 – 1,100.00, paid $ _____

Sunshine is dressed in a black and white checkered dress with sunflower accents and an eyelet apron. She is wearing a black and white checkered straw hat with sunflowers on it.

☐ **MAGGIE**
   #1606
Issued 1995, Date purchased _____
Limited 1,000, 26" tall
Market value: $275.00 – 300.00, paid $ _____

Maggie wears a calico and blue plaid dress with eyelet lace trim. She has long-legged bloomers and a dust cap that matches the dress. Her bag and shoes are made of burlap.

☐ **VALERIE**
   #1607
Issued 1996, Date purchased _____
Limited 1,000, 26" tall
Market value: $250.00 – 275.00, paid $ _____

Valerie is dressed in a ladybug and flower printed pinafore dress accented with cream and green checkered material. She is wearing a cute hat on her head.

"PRETTY AS A PICTURE" SERIES

☐ **ROCHELLE**
#1380
Issued 1999, Date purchased _____
Limited 50,000, 12" tall
Market value: $29.95, paid $_____

Rochelle wears a maroon crushed velvet dress with pink sleeves. She is carrying an umbrella. She was the second doll in the "Pretty As A Picture" series for the QVC television network.

☐ **JANELLE**
#1480
Issued 1997, Date purchased _____
Limited 50,000, 12" tall
Market value: $35.00 – 50.00, paid $ _____

Janelle is dressed in a pink long-sleeved dress accented with silver trim. She is carrying a garden basket of roses and white flowers. She was the first doll in the "Pretty As A Picture" series for the QVC television network.

PUBLISHER'S CLEARING HOUSE EXCLUSIVE

☐ **CINDY**
#1441
Issued 1996, Date purchased _____
Limited 10,000, 12" tall
Market value: $29.95, paid $ _____

Cindy comes in bluish-purple flower printed coveralls with a pink sweater. She is carrying a pink blanket. She comes with a certificate of authenticity that says she was produced as a Publisher's Clearing House exclusive.

PUPPET SERIES

These cute little dolls are each wrapped in a cozy blanket equipped with a hole in the bottom for use as a puppet.

☐ **GIRL PUPPET**
#1798
Issued 2001, Date purchased ——————
Current, 12" tall
Market value: $21.00, paid $——————

☐ **BOY PUPPET**
#1799
Issued 2001, Date purchased ——————
Current, 12" tall
Market value: $21.00, paid $ ——————

QVC EXCLUSIVES

☐ **NICOLAS**
#1042
Issued 1993, Date purchased ——————————
Limited 40,000, 16" tall
Market value: $175.00 – 200.00, paid $ ——————————

Nicolas is a blue-eyed curly blond boy that is dressed in a red sleeper with a red Santa hat. He comes in a red stocking with a plaid patch. Nicholas was the first in the "Stocking" series for QVC.

☐ **NICOLE**
#1056
Issued 1994, Date purchased ——————————
Limited 40,000, 16" tall
Market value: $125.00 – 150.00, paid $ ——————

Nicole has her long brunette hair in two braids and has green eyes. She is wearing red flannel pajamas and a red stocking cap and comes in a red stocking. She is the second in the "Stocking" series for QVC.

NOEL
#1073
Issued 1996, Date purchased _____
Limited 50,000, 16" tall
Market value: $100.00 – 125.00, paid $ _____

Noel models her long brunette hair in one braid down her back and is wearing a plaid cap/beret with matching plaid pajamas. She fits nicely in a red stocking. She is the fourth edition in the "Stocking" series for QVC.

NIKKI
#1087
Issued 1995, Date purchased _____
Limited 40,000, 16" tall
Market value: $100.00 – 125.00, paid $ _____

Nikki has her long blond hair in two braids and is wearing red flannel pajamas and a red stocking cap. She fits well in a red stocking, and has freckles. She is the third edition in the "Stocking" series for QVC.

CHRISTMAS CAROL
#1091
Issued 2000, Date purchased _____
Limited 60,000, 16" tall
Market value: $39.00 – 45.00, paid $ _____

Carol has dark blond hair and is dressed in white and green pajamas. She comes in a green stocking with a patch on it. She is the eighth edition in the "Stocking" series for QVC.

LINDSAY
#1105
Issued 1996, Date purchased _____
Limited one time sale, 16" tall
Market value: $75.00 – 100.00, paid $ _____

Lindsay comes in a cream taffeta and lace dress with yellow, pink, and mint satin ribbons. She was sold on QVC during one television appearance.

JINGLES
#1113
Issued 1997, Date purchased _____
Limited 50,000, 16" tall
Market value: $75.00 – 85.00, paid $ _____

Jingles wears her blond hair straight and cropped. She is wearing plaid night clothes and a red stocking cap and comes in a red stocking. She is the fifth edition in the "Stocking" series for QVC.

MIRANDA
#1124
Issued 2000, Date purchased _____
Limited 1,500, 16" tall
Market value: $45.00 – 50.00, paid $ _____

Miranda has blond curls and blue eyes and is wearing a beautiful light blue gown adorned with white lace. She carries a basket of flowers and has a matching hat on her head.

KATE
#1125
Issued 2000, Date purchased _____
Limited 1,500, 16" tall
Market value: $39.95, paid $_____

Kate is a blond ballerina wearing a pretty pink tutu. She is wearing matching pink dance shoes and has her hair pulled up in the back with flowers.

CHRISTMAS EVE
#1132
Issued 1998, Date purchased _____
Limited 60,000, 16" tall
Market value: $60.00 – 75.00, paid $ _____

Eve wears her blond hair in two braids and is wearing a pretty green holiday dress and a red stocking cap. She comes in a red stocking. She is the sixth edition in the "Stocking" series for QVC.

☐ **HOLLY**
#1141
Issued 1999, Date purchased _____
Limited 60,000, 16" tall
Market value: $60.00 – 75.00, paid $ _____

Holly has long curly and wavy red hair and is wearing a pretty red and white satin dress. She comes in a green stocking with a plaid patch. She is the seventh edition in the "Stocking" series for QVC.

☐ **JULES**
#1209
Issued 1999, Date purchased _____
Limited 1,000, 26" tall
Market value: $250.00 – 275.00, paid $ _____

Jules has purple hair and green eyes. He is dressed in a fun green and purple clown outfit with a matching hat.

☐ **ANGEL**
#1311
Issued 1999, Date purchased _____
Limited 3,000, 12" tall
Market value: $39.00 – 45.00, paid $ _____

Angel has dark blond hair in two little ponytails and is wearing a pink satin and white lace dress. She has a pink satin bonnet on her head. She was issued for the 10th anniversary of Precious Moments Company.

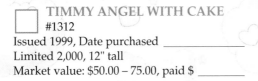

☐ **TIMMY ANGEL WITH CAKE**
#1312
Issued 1999, Date purchased _____
Limited 2,000, 12" tall
Market value: $50.00 – 75.00, paid $ _____

Timmy has blond hair with a golden halo in it. He is wearing a white angelic gown. He was issued for the 10th anniversary of the Precious Moments Chapel.

LAURA & LIZA
#1410
Issued 1996, Date purchased _____
Limited 9,000, 12" tall
Market value: 100.00 – 125.00, paid $ _____

Laura & Liza are twins wearing heart print navy blouses with contrasting tan and navy heart print dresses and hats.

LITTLE CHRISTMAS CAROL
#1675
Issued 2000, Date purchased _____
Current, 7" tall
Market value: $12.95, paid $ _____

Little Christmas Carol has dark blond hair with a green hat accented with red flowers. She is wearing a white top and green and red plaid dress accented with red flowers. She has matching shoes with red flower accents.

LITTLE HOLLY
#1679
Issued 1999, Date purchased _____
Current, 7" tall
Market value: $59.95, paid $_____

Holly has long curly and wavy red hair and is wearing a pretty red and white satin dress. She wears a matching hat.

RAINBOW BABIES SERIES

☐ **PINK BABY**
#1801
Issued 2002, Date purchased _____
Current, 12" tall
Market value: $10.00, paid $ _____

Pink Baby is dressed in soft pink, terrycloth pajamas with a hood. On the right side of the pajamas is an embroidered rainbow.

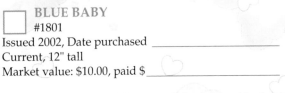

☐ **BLUE BABY**
#1801
Issued 2002, Date purchased _____
Current, 12" tall
Market value: $10.00, paid $_____

Blue Baby is dressed in soft blue, terrycloth pajamas with a hood. On the right side of the pajamas is an embroidered rainbow.

☐ **BLUE BABY**
#1803
Issued 2002, Date purchased _____
Current, 16" tall
Market value: $20.00, paid $_____

Blue Baby is dressed in soft blue, terrycloth pajamas with a hood. On the pajamas is an embroidered rainbow. This baby comes with a white bib that can be personalized.

☐ **PINK BABY**
#1803
Issued 2002, Date purchased _____
Current, 16" tall
Market value: $20.00, paid $_____

Pink Baby is dressed in soft pink, terrycloth pajamas with a hood. On the pajamas is an embroidered rainbow. This baby comes with a white bib that can be personalized.

ROSES IN BLOOM

ROSA LINDA
#1152
Issued October 2002, Date purchased _____
Current, 16" tall
Market value: $48.00, paid $_____

Rosa Linda has curly blond hair with a pink flower effect around her head. She is wearing a cute pink dress with a black bow around her waistline. She has a pink ribbon around her left ankle.

ROSE MARIE
#4233
Issued October 2002, Date purchased _____
Current, 12" tall
Market value: $36.00, paid $_____

Rose Marie has curly black hair with a pink flower effect around her head. She is wearing a cute pink dress with a black bow around her waistline. She has a pink ribbon around her left ankle.

ROSIE
#4234
Issued October 2002, Date purchased _____
Current, 12" tall
Market value: $36.00, paid $_____

Rosie has curly brown hair with a cream-colored flower effect around her head. She is wearing a cute cream-colored dress with a black bow around her waistline. She has a cream-colored ribbon around her left ankle.

ROSANNA
#4235
Issued October 2002, Date purchased _____
Current, 12" tall
Market value: $36.00, paid $_____

Rosanna has curly black hair with a pink flower effect around her head. She is wearing a cute pink dress with a black bow around her waistline and a pink ribbon around her left ankle.

"SONGS OF THE SPIRIT" SERIES

☐ **FAITH**
#1076
Issued 1995,
Date purchased _____
Suspended 1998, 16" tall
Market value: $50.00 – 75.00,
paid $_____

Faith is dressed in a lavender and light blue gown covered in white lace. Faith has long wavy blond hair and blue eyes. She is carrying a little harp.

☐ **LOVE**
#1077
Issued 1995,
Date purchased _____
Suspended 1998, 16" tall
Market value: $50.00 – 75.00,
paid $_____

Love has long wavy brunette hair and green eyes. She is dressed in a long pink gown and is carrying a violin.

☐ **CHARITY**
#1079
Issued 1995,
Date purchased _____
Suspended 1998, 16" tall
Market value: $50.00 – 75.00,
paid $_____

Charity is dressed in a light blue satin dress. She has pretty blond hair and blue eyes. She is carrying a French horn.

☐ **HOPE**
#1078
Issued 1995,
Date purchased _____
Suspended 1998, 16" tall
Market value: $50.00 – 75.00,
paid $_____

Hope is dressed in a yellow satin gown and has dark blond hair and brown eyes. She is carrying a trumpet.

SINGAPORE EXCLUSIVES

These dolls have black hair with a flower off to the right side. They are dressed in a multicolored flower print dress native to their country.

☐ **MEI RONG**

Issued 1999, Date purchased _____
Exclusive to Singapore, 12" tall
Market value: $29.95, paid $_____

☐ SHU FEN

Issued 1999, Date purchased _____
Exclusive to Singapore, 9" tall
Market value: $12.95, paid $_____

SPIEGEL CATALOG EXCLUSIVES

☐ **GLORIA**
  #2012
Issued 1996, Date purchased _____
Limited to one catalog, 12" tall
Market value: $75.00 – 85.00, paid $_____

Gloria is a pretty little tree topper dressed in a white angelic gown with gold trim. She has dark blond hair. She was limited for sale in one catalog only.

☐ **CASSANDRA**
  #2016
Issued 1997, Date purchased _____
Limited to one catalog, 12" tall
Market value: $50.00, paid $_____

Cassandra is a pretty little tree topper dressed in a white angelic gown with gold trim. She has dark blond hair. She was limited for sale in one catalog only.

☐ **GWENDOLENE**
#4224
Issued October 2002,
Date purchased _____
Current, 12" tall
Market value: $42.00, paid $ _____

Gwendolene is dressed in a beautiful mint green lacy gown with flower accents. She has long curly black hair with a mint green princess hat.

☐ **GWYNETH**
#4225
Issued October 2002,
Date purchased _____
Current, 12" tall
Market value: $42.00, paid $ _____

Gwyneth is dressed in a beautiful white lacy gown with flower accents. She has long curly brown hair with a white princess hat.

☐ **GUINEVERE**
#4226
Issued October 2002,
Date purchased _____
Current, 12" tall
Market value: $42.00, paid $ _____

Guinevere is dressed in a beautiful pink lacy gown with flower accents. She has long curly blond hair with a pink princess hat.

"STRIKE UP THE BAND" SERIES

☐ **MAJORETTE**
#1379
Issued July 1998, Date purchased _____
Suspended September 2000, 12" tall
Market value: $29.95, paid $_____

Majorette is wearing a white and gold satin uniform with matching hat, a pair of white marching boots, and carries a baton. She has long dark blond curly hair and blue eyes. Majorette is the first edition in the series.

☐ **BATON TWIRLER**
#1380
Issued September 1998, Date purchased _____
Suspended September 2000, 12" tall
Market value: $29.95, paid $ _____

Baton Twirler has straight dark blond hair and wears a white satin uniform with lavender trim that includes matching boots. She is carrying a baton. Baton Twirler is the second edition in the series.

☐ **FLAG GIRL**
#1381
Issued January 1999, Date purchased _____
Suspended September 2000, 12" tall
Market value: $29.95, paid $_____

Flag Girl has straight brunette hair and wears a white satin uniform with light blue trim that includes matching boots and a hat. She is carrying a light blue flag. Flag girl is the third edition in the series.

☐ **BAND MEMBER**
#1382
Issued April 1999, Date purchased _____
Suspended September 2000, 12" tall
Market value: $29.95, paid $_____

Band Member has curly brunette hair and is wearing a white satin uniform with light green trim that includes matching boots and a hat. She is carrying a clarinet. Band member is the fourth edition in the series.

ALYSSA
#1333
Issued January 2000, Date purchased _____
Current, 12" tall
Market value: $29.95, paid $ _____

Alyssa has straight blond hair that is pulled back in two ponytails and big blue eyes. She is wearing a pretty set of yellow pajamas with matching slippers. She is carrying her favorite "Precious" stuffed lamb.

JOSIE
#1334
Issued January 2000, Date purchased _____
Current, 12" tall
Market value: $29.95, paid $ _____

Josie has straight dark blond hair that is pulled back into two ponytails and big blue eyes. She is wearing a pretty set of white pajamas with matching slippers. She is carrying her favorite "Precious" stuffed pink bunny.

SADIE
#1335
Issued January 2000, Date purchased _____
Current, 12" tall
Market value: $29.95, paid $ _____

Sadie has straight red hair that is pulled back in two ponytails, big green eyes, and bright and cheery freckles. She is wearing a set of green pajamas with matching slippers. She is carrying her favorite "Precious" stuffed green puppy dog.

BRENNA
#1336
Issued January 2000, Date purchased _____
Current, 12" tall
Market value: $29.95, paid $ _____

Brenna has straight brunette hair that is pulled back with a
pretty blue headband, big brown eyes, and adorable wire glasses.
She is wearing a set of blue pajamas with matching slippers.
She is carrying her favorite "Precious" stuffed yellow pony.

CALLIE
#1337
Issued January 2000, Date purchased _____
Current, 12" tall
Market value: $29.95, paid $_____

Callie has straight blond hair that is pulled back into a
side ponytail, and big blue eyes. She is wearing a pretty
set of pink pajamas with matching slippers. She is carrying her favorite "Precious" stuffed teddy bear.

BETTY JO
#4218
Issued August 2002, Date purchased _____
Current, 12" tall
Market value: $30.00, paid $_____

Betty Jo is dressed for a good night's sleep in her blue and
white polka dot pajamas. She has long black hair with
blue ribbons. She is carrying a yellow and blue stuffed
elephant.

☐ **BENITA**
#4219
Issued August 2002, Date purchased _____
Current, 12" tall
Market value: $30.00, paid $ _____

Benita is dressed for a good night's sleep in her light green gown with a matching cap. She has long black hair in ponytails with light green ribbons. She is carrying her favorite stuffed monkey.

☐ **BECCA**
#4220
Issued August 2002, Date purchased _____
Current, 12" tall
Market value: $30.00, paid $ _____

Becca is dressed for bed in her pink pajamas and pink slippers. She has long blond hair with a pink and white bow in it. She is carrying a light green pig.

☐ **BONNIE**
#4221
Issued August 2002, Date purchased _____
Current, 12" tall
Market value: $30.00, paid $ _____

Bonnie is ready for bed in her yellow and lavender polka dot sleep gown. She has curly blond hair with a yellow ribbon around it and glasses. She is carrying her favorite stuffed lion.

SWEETHEART SERIES

RACHEL
#1029
Issued 1991, Date purchased _____
Retired 1993, 16" tall
Market value: $225.00 – 250.00, paid $ _____

Rachel has long wavy brunette hair that is partially pulled back with a big red bow. This green-eyed doll wears a red and white long gown that is trimmed with white lace, red shoes with golden buckles, and a heart-shaped locket. Rachel is the first edition in the series.

EMILY
#1037
Issued 1992, Date purchased _____
1 year production, 16" tall
Market value: $200.00 – 225.00, paid $ _____

Emily has big beautiful long blond curly hair that is pulled back a bit with a blue floral headband. She has big blue eyes and carries a soft satin pink pillow. Emily wears a long white dress with pink lace trim and a necklace. Emily is the second edition in the series.

MAKENZIE
#1049
Issued 1999, Date purchased _____
1 year production, 16" tall
Market value: $75.00 – 100.00, paid $ _____

Makenzie has beautiful dark blond hair that is pulled up in a festive fashion with a pink bow fastener. She is carrying a heart-shaped floral wreath. She wears a fancy pink dress that is trimmed with faux pearls. Makenzie is the eighth and last edition in the series.

AMBER
#1053
Issued 1994, Date purchased _____
1 year production, 16" tall
Market value: $200.00 – 225.00, paid $ _____

Amber has long wavy blond hair and wears an ornate pink dress with a white petticoat, white lace pantyhose, and lace gloves. She has a big pink bow in her hair. Amber is the third edition in the series.

☐ **HANNAH**
#1061
Issued 1997, Date purchased _____
1 year production, 16" tall
Market value: $100.00 – 125.00, paid $ _____

Hannah has long blond hair that is pulled back with a white satin headband. She is wearing a long ornate white satin dress with a sheer overlay printed with tiny pink hearts. Hannah is the sixth edition in the series.

☐ **COURTNEY**
#1083
Issued 1995, Date purchased _____
1 year production, 16" tall
Market value: $125.00 – 150.00, paid $ _____

Courtney has blond wavy hair and blue eyes. She is wearing a long pink print dress with white lace trim. She is carrying a small white book that says "Love" on the cover. Courtney is the fourth edition in the series.

☐ **ROSEMARY**
#1090
Issued 1996, Date purchased _____
1 year production, 16" tall
Market value: $100.00 – 125.00, paid $ _____

Rosemary has gorgeous long brunette/auburn curly hair that is pulled back a bit with a red bow, and big green eyes (with green eyeshadow accents). She is carrying a red rose. Rosemary wears a bright red rose print dress. Rosemary is the fifth edition in the series.

☐ **CHLOE**
#1119
Issued 1998, Date purchased _____
1 year production, 16" tall
Market value: $50.00 – 75.00, paid $ _____

Chloe has long straight brunette hair that is partially pulled back into a pretty braid and fastened with a big red bow. She is wearing a soft satin red dress that is trimmed with white lace and matching red shoes. Chloe is the seventh edition in the series.

TEN LITTLE INDIANS SERIES

These Indians are dressed in their traditional native outfits. This series is complete with the teepee.

☐ **ONE LITTLE INDIAN**
  #1680
Issued 2000, Date purchased _____
Current, 7" tall
Market value: $12.00, paid $_____

☐ **TWO LITTLE INDIAN**
  #1681
Issued 2000, Date purchased _____
Current, 7" tall
Market value: $12.00, paid $_____

☐ **THREE LITTLE INDIAN**
  #1682
Issued 2000, Date purchased _____
Current, 7" tall
Market value: $12.00, paid $_____

☐ **FOUR LITTLE INDIAN**
  #1683
Issued 2000, Date purchased _____
Current, 7" tall
Market value: $12.00, paid $_____

FIVE LITTLE INDIAN
#1684
Issued 2000, Date purchased _____
Current, 7" tall
Market value: $12.00, paid $ _____

SIX LITTLE INDIAN
#1685
Issued 2000, Date purchased _____
Current, 7" tall
Market value: $12.00, paid $ _____

SEVEN LITTLE INDIAN
#1686
Issued 2000, Date purchased _____
Current, 7" tall
Market value: $12.00, paid $ _____

EIGHT LITTLE INDIAN
#1687
Issued 2000, Date purchased _____
Current, 7" tall
Market value: $12.00, paid $ _____

☐ **NINE LITTLE INDIAN**
#1688
Issued 2000, Date purchased _____
Current, 7" tall
Market value: $12.00, paid $ _____

☐ **TEN LITTLE INDIAN**
#1689
Issued 2000, Date purchased _____
Current, 7" tall
Market value: $12.00, paid $ _____

☐ **TEEPEE**
#1690
Issued 2000, Date purchased _____
Current, 7" tall
Market value: $4.00, paid $ _____

BLOND GROOM
#1284
Issued October 2002, Date purchased _____
Current, 16" tall
Market value: $60.00, paid $ _____

Groom is dressed for his wedding in a black tuxedo, black bow tie, and white shirt. He also has a black top hat on his head of blond hair.

BLOND BRIDE
#1285
Issued October 2002, Date purchased _____
Current, 16" tall
Market value: $100.00, paid $ _____

Bride is dressed for her special day in a long white wedding gown with flower accents. She has long curly blond hair that is carrying her long white veil.

BRIDESMAID
#1286
Issued October 2002, Date purchased _____
Current, 16" tall
Market value: $85.00, paid $ _____

Bridesmaid is dressed in a long pink and white lacy gown with flower accents. She has long straight hair with a big white bow on the top of her head.

FLOWER GIRL
#4230
Issued October 2002, Date purchased _____
Current, 12" tall
Market value: $38.00, paid $ _____

Flower girl is dressed in a long pink and white lacy gown with flower accents. She has long curly blond hair with a large bow on the top of her head.

☐ **BRIDE**
#1287
Issued October 2002,
Date purchased _____
Current, 16" tall
Market value: $100.00, paid $ _____

Bride is dressed for her special day in a long white wedding gown with flower acents. She has long curly auburn hair and a long white veil.

☐ **GROOM**
#1288
Issued October 2002, Date purchased _____
Current, 16" tall
Market value: $60.00, paid $ _____

Groom is dressed for his wedding in a black tuxedo, black bow tie, and white shirt. He also has a black top hat on his head of auburn hair.

☐ **BRIDE**
#1289
Issued October 2002,
Date purchased _____
Current, 16" tall
Market value: $100.00, paid $ _____

Bride is dressed for her special day in a long white wedding gown with flower acents. She has long curly dark brown hair and a long white veil.

☐ **GROOM**
#1290
Issued October 2002, Date purchased _____
Current, 16" tall
Market value: $60.00, paid $ _____

Groom is dressed for his wedding in a black tuxedo, black bow tie, and white shirt. He also has a black top hat on his head of dark brown hair.

THE FIRST KISS SERIES

GEORGIA
#4222
Issued October 2002, Date purchased _____
Current, 12" tall
Market value: $36.00, paid $ _____

Georgia has long curly blond hair with a large pink bow in it. She is wearing a long pink gown trimmed in white lace.

GARRETT
#4223
Issued October 2002, Date purchased _____
Current, 12" tall
Market value: $29.50, paid $ _____

Garrett is dressed in a pair of black slacks held up with black suspenders and a white shirt accented with a pink bow tie. On his head is a black top hat accented with a pink ribbon. He is carrying a bouquet of flowers.

TOOTY FRUITY SERIES

STRAWBERRY SHAY
#4245
Issued October 2002, Date purchased _____
Current, 12" tall
Market value: $32.00, paid $ _____

Strawberry Shay has pretty blond hair in ponytails with red ribbons. She is dressed in a strawberry and green leaves accented dress with white trim. She has a matching hat on her head and is carrying a strawberry.

CANDY APPLE
#4246
Issued October 2002, Date purchased _____
Current, 12" tall
Market value: $32.00, paid $ _____

Candy Apple has brown curly hair with a straw hat with red apples. She is wearing a green plaid and white jumper with red apple accents. She is carrying a red apple.

WENDY WATERMELON
#4247
Issued October 2002, Date purchased _____
Current, 12" tall
Market value: $32.00, paid $_____

Wendy Watermelon is dressed in a pair of red and white striped coveralls with watermelon shaped appliqués. She has short blond hair with a large watermelon shaped bow on her head. She is carrying a slice of watermelon.

VICTORIAN SERIES

OLIVIA
#1054
Issued 1999, Date purchased _____
1 year production, 16" tall
Market value: $75.00 – 100.00, paid $_____

Olivia is wearing a long mauve and maroon dress with floral print accents. She wears her hair up and wears a Victorian style hat that matches her dress. She is carrying a matching umbrella.

ELIZABETH
#1123
Issued 1998, Date purchased _____
1 year production, 16" tall
Market value: $125.00 – 150.00, paid $_____

Elizabeth has long dark golden blond hair styled with a cameo and dark blue ribbon. She is wearing a long crushed velvet dress in a midnight blue color trimmed with lace. She is carrying a matching purse.

ALEXANDRIA
#1142
Issued 2000, Date purchased _____
1 year production, 16" tall
Market value: $49.95, paid $_____

Alexandria has brown eyes and brunette hair that is pulled up and braided. She is wearing a long green velvet dress and holding a feather fan.

VICKY
#1149
Issued 2001, Date purchased _____
1 year production, 16" tall
Market value: $49.95, paid $_____

Vicky has pretty black hair and green eyes. She is wearing a gorgeous burgundy, pink, and cream satin gown. She is carrying a purse.

WELCOME HOME BABY

These babies are fully dressed in soft flannel sleepers and each comes with its own flannel blanket with satin trim. They come packaged in painted wooden cradles.

☐ **YELLOW**
#1780
Issued 1992, Date purchased _____
Discontinued 1994, 6" tall
Market value: $65.00 – 75.00, paid $_____

☐ **BLUE**
#1781
Issued 1992, Date purchased _____
Discontinued 1994, 6" tall
Market value: $65.00 – 75.00, paid $_____

☐ **PINK**
#1782
Issued 1992, Date purchased _____
Discontinued 1994, 6" tall
Market value: $65.00 – 75.00, paid $_____

WOODEN DOLL SERIES

Louise and Fredrick are wooden dolls. They are musical and play "Edelweiss." They come on wooden bases with their names on plaques. They were the first editions in the series.

☐ **LOUISE**
#1218
Issued 1996, Date purchased _____
Limited 1,000, 12" tall
Market value: $750.00 – 1,000.00, paid $_____

☐ **FREDRICK**
#1219
Issued 1996, Date purchased _____
Limited 1,000, 12" tall
Market value: $750.00 – 1,000.00, paid $_____

Natasha and Gertrude are wooden dolls. They are musical and play "God Bless America." They come on wooden bases with their names on plaques. They were the second editions in the series.

☐ **NATASHA (BRUNETTE)**
#1231
Issued 1997, Date purchased _____
Limited 1,000, 12" tall
Market value: $500.00 – 550.00, paid $_____

☐ **GERTRUDE (BLOND)**
#1232
Issued 1997, Date purchased _____
Limited 1,000, 12" tall
Market value: $500.00 – 550.00, paid $_____

Rene and Ryan are sailors, made of wood and dressed in blue. They are musical dolls playing "Anchors Away." They come on wooden bases with their names on plaques. They were the third editions in the series.

☐ **RENE**
#1233
Issued 1998, Date purchased _____
Limited 1,000, 12" tall
Market value: $250.00 – 275.00, paid $_____

☐ **RYAN**
#1234
Issued 1998, Date purchased _____
Limited 1,000, 12" tall
Market value: $250.00 – 275.00, paid $_____

GLOSSARY

Closed — status for limited edition pieces that are no longer produced.

Discontinued — collectibles which have been permanently removed from production and there are no plans to produce these items again. These collectibles were not given the prestigious status of "Retired."

Limited Edition — collectibles that are limited by a specific number produced, limited by being produced for one year, limited by being produced for two years, or limited to being produced for a specific event.

Numbered Edition — open edition pieces that are numbered.

One Year Production — a doll produced for only one year.

Retired — collectibles that are no longer being produced by the manufacturer.

Secondary Market/Dealers — collectibles that are not readily available at retail stores because they are no longer being produced and have sold out. These items are said to be "secondary market" items. The "Secondary Market Dealers" are those dealers who buy back individual collectibles or entire collections to resell them.

Series — group of collectibles which have a common theme.

Suspended — collectibles that have been removed from production for an unspecified period of time. There is no time limit on how long the collectible can be suspended from production.

Variations — collectibles that undergo a major production design changes.

INDEX BY SERIES

General Index

NUMERICAL INDEX

MY PRECIOUS NOTES

Name of Doll _____

☐ Retired/☐ Suspended/☐ Limited in production/☐ Current

Issued _____ / Date purchased _____

Market value _____ / paid _____

Name of Doll _____

☐ Retired/☐ Suspended/☐ Limited in production/☐ Current

Issued _____ / Date purchased _____

Market value _____ / paid _____

Name of Doll _____

☐ Retired/☐ Suspended/☐ Limited in production/☐ Current

Issued _____ / Date purchased _____

Market value _____ / paid _____

Name of Doll _____

☐ Retired/☐ Suspended/☐ Limited in production/☐ Current

Issued _____ / Date Purchased _____

Market value _____ / paid _____

Name of Doll _____

☐ Retired/☐ Suspended/☐ Limited in production/☐ Current

Issued _____ / Date purchased _____

Market value _____ / paid _____

Name of Doll _____

☐ Retired/☐ Suspended/☐ Limited in production/☐ Current

Issued _____ / Date purchased _____

Market value _____ / paid _____

Name of Doll _____

☐ Retired/☐ Suspended/☐ Limited in production/☐ Current

Issued _____ / Date purchased _____

Market value _____ / paid _____

Name of Doll _____

☐ Retired/☐ Suspended/☐ Limited in production/☐ Current

Issued _____ / Date purchased _____

Market value _____ / paid _____

Name of Doll _____

☐ Retired/☐ Suspended/☐ Limited in production/☐ Current

Issued _____ / Date Purchased _____

Market value _____ / paid _____

Name of Doll _____

☐ Retired/☐ Suspended/☐ Limited in production/☐ Current

Issued _____ / Date purchased _____

Market value _____ / paid _____

Name of Doll _____

☐ Retired/☐ Suspended/☐ Limited in production/☐ Current

Issued _____ / Date purchased _____

Market value _____ / paid _____

Name of Doll _____

☐ Retired/☐ Suspended/☐ Limited in production/☐ Current

Issued _____ / Date purchased _____

Market value _____ / paid _____

Name of Doll _____

☐ Retired/☐ Suspended/☐ Limited in production/☐ Current

Issued _____ / Date purchased _____

Market value _____ / paid _____

Name of Doll _____

☐ Retired/☐ Suspended/☐ Limited in production/☐ Current

Issued _____ / Date Purchased _____

Market value _____ / paid _____

Name of Doll _____

☐ Retired/☐ Suspended/☐ Limited in production/☐ Current

Issued _____ / Date purchased _____

Market value _____ / paid _____

Name of Doll _____

☐ Retired/☐ Suspended/☐ Limited in production/☐ Current

Issued _____ / Date purchased _____

Market value _____ /paid _____

Name of Doll _____

☐ Retired/☐ Suspended/☐ Limited in production/☐ Current

Issued _____ / Date purchased _____

Market value _____ / paid _____

Name of Doll _____

☐ Retired/☐ Suspended/☐ Limited in production/☐ Current

Issued _____ / Date purchased _____

Market value _____ / paid _____

Name of Doll _____

☐ Retired/☐ Suspended/☐ Limited in production/☐ Current

Issued _____ / Date Purchased _____

Market value _____ / paid _____

Name of Doll _____

☐ Retired/☐ Suspended/☐ Limited in production/☐ Current

Issued _____ / Date purchased _____

Market value _____ / paid _____